Score More

A self help book to help students excel

Rohit Shetty

First Published in India in 2015 by First Step Publishing

Editorial / Sales / Marketing Office at
303-304 Garnet Nirmal Lifestyles Ph 2
Behind Nirmal Lifestyles Mall
LBS Marg Mulund West
Mumbai 400080
E-Mail:- info@firststepcorp.com
www.firststepcorp.com

ISBN: - 978-93-83306-29-9
Publisher and Managing Editor: Rohit Shetty
Branding, Marketing and Promotions by: Design Fishing
Digital Management by: First Step Corp
Typeset in Book Antique
PaperBack: ₹ 499 India
Rest $10

Table Of Content

Step Twelve

Creative Visualization

And

Imagination

Success strategies to be a top scorer

Lakshya–developing your goals

Your Goals must be SMART

Time Management

Power of Concentration

Exercise1

Exercise2

W - Write.

Strategy for Solving Math Word Problems

R - Read

Q - Question

W - Write

Q - Question

C - Compute

Q - Question

M-U-R-D-E-R Study Technique

Mood–

Understand–

Recall-

Digest–

Expand –

Review–

Do's and Don'ts tips for academic success

Writers Note

Introduction

Welcome!

First of all let me thank you as it's my great pleasure and honour to share with you the secret of a Genius which I happened to observe whilst teaching and counselling academically more than 1000 students over a decade and from wide range of scientific materials.

So is it the book or just another book? Answer to that you will find out once you are done reading this book. This book is easy to understand and down to earth format. Tricks and strategies are simple and consumes less time. Wherever possible stories has been included to explain my point in the best way. This book speaks directly to you as if I were talking to you so as to keep communication healthy.

This book is not meant for one time reading. Instead this book is like a coach guiding you towards the path of success. Infact, I would advise you to read it once and then re-read it periodically to check yourself whether you are walking on the right track. So before you read further please stop and keep a pen or pencil handy so that you can track your progress. Mark of a Genius is penning down the random thoughts and then mule over it's different interpretations.

With just a pen and paper, Einstein peeked farther behind Nature's curtain than anyone had since Newton, then spent the rest of his years living it down. Genius people steer their life towards success. They always keep the steering control with themselves rather than leaving at the mercy of destiny.

Let me share a beautiful incident which occurred with me on one fine day –

When I was in my college, I use to commute with my bike to college everyday and one of my friend use to accompany with me .One day when I was about to leave for college, my friend requested me that he wants to ride my bike to college. I said well, fine but be very careful while riding.

He accelerated the bike and suddenly I felt uneasiness. This was the first time I was a pillion rider and was getting scared as my friend started taking horrendous twist and turns. Fate it seems, We met with an accident but fortunately nothing happened to both of us. Somehow we reached college and I was completely in a horrified state. That night I was wondering why was I so afraid? I realized that it was feeling of not being under control, was the cause of me being afraid!

My dear students, it is this attitude of being under control which gives you full control over your life and studies. Most students are like a pillion rider, they depend on their teacher, their friends and are waiting for these people to take twist and turns of their life by giving them entire control of their life rather than being under control and when suddenly they hit dead end down the road then they use a special tactics of blame game. Few blame their luck, financial problem, knowledge etc and other external circumstances. Some students say that they really did the hard work but still can't score. Some student study only when a test has been announced otherwise they wait and enjoy unless the teacher declares a test giving entire control of your life and studies to the teacher. You might as well want to create your list of blame, go ahead and create a stupid list for yourself. If not then let's continue.

Now, you should understand that a teacher is like a guide who will show you the right path but it is YOU who has to ride all the way to your goals. It's time to take control of your life and studies. Now the Question in your mind must be, "How do I take full control of my life and studies? Well it all starts with your Attitude & Discipline.

Let me give you a Simple Formula to make your Life 100% successful...

If
A B CD E FG H I J K LM N O P Q R ST U V WX Y Z
Is equal to
1 2 3 4 5 6 7 8 9 10 11 12 13 14 15 16 17 18 19 20 21 22 23 24 25 26.

Then,
H+A+R+D+W+O+R+K = 8+1+18+4+23+15+18+11 =98%
K+N+O+W+L+E+D+G+E = 11+14+15+23+12+5+4+7+5 = 96%
L+O+V+E=12+15+22+5=54%
L+U+C+K = 12+21+3+11 = 47%

None of them makes 100%...
Then what makes 100%? Is it Money? ...
...No!!!!! Luck?...
...NO!!!!

Every problem has a solution, only if we perhaps change our

"ATTITUDE"
It is OUR ATTITUDE towards Life and Work that makes... OUR Life
100% Successful...

You see
A+T+T+I+T+U+D+E= 1+20+20+9+20+21+4+5 = 100%

To achieve this 100%attitude, you must!!! Be DISCIPLINED in
life......yes that reminds me...Even

D+I+S+C+I+P+L+I+N+E = 100%

Don't you think so?

We will be discussing more about attitude and discipline in the chapter's
ahead

Let's read about thought pattern of a Genius --

The university professor challenged his students with this question.

Did God create everything that exists?
A student bravely replied yes, he did!"
"God created everything?"The professor asked. "Yes, sir," the student replied.

The professor answered, "If God created everything, then God created evil since evil exists, and according to the principal that our works define who we are then God is evil."
The student became quiet before such an answer.
The professor was quite pleased with himself and boasted to the students that he had proven once more that the Christian faith was a myth.
Another student raised his hand and said, "Can I ask you a question professor?" "Of course", replied the professor. The student stood up and asked, "Professor does cold exist?"
"What kind of question is this? Of course it exists. Have you never been cold?" The students snickered at the young man's question.
The young man replied, "In fact sir, cold does not exist. According to the laws of physics, what we consider cold is in reality the absence of heat. Everybody and every object is susceptible to study when it has or transmits energy, and heat is what makes a body or matter have or transmit energy. Absolute zero (- 460 degrees F) is the total absence of heat; all matter becomes inert and incapable of reaction at that temperature. Cold does not exist. We have created this word to describe how we feel if we have too little heat.
The student continued. "Professor, does darkness exist?" The professor responded, "Of course it does".
The student replied, "Once again you are wrong sir, darkness does not exist either. Darkness is in reality the absence of light. Light we can study, but not darkness. In fact we can use Newton's prism to break

white light into many colours and study the various wavelengths of each colour. You cannot measure darkness. A simple ray of light can break into a world of darkness and illuminate it. How can you know how dark a certain space is? You measure the amount of light present. Isn't this correct? Darkness is a term used by man to describe what happens when there is no light present."

Finally the young man asked the professor. "Sir, does evil exist?" Now uncertain, the professor responded, "Of course as I have already said. We see it every day. It is in the daily example of man's inhumanity to man. It is in the multitude of crime and violence everywhere in the world. "These manifestations are nothing else but evil."

To this the student replied, "Evil does not exist sir, or atleast it does not exist unto itself. Evil is simply the absence of God. It is just like darkness and cold, a word that man has created to describe the absence of God. God did not create evil. Evil is not like faith, or love, that exist just as does light and heat. Evil is the result of what happens when man does not have God's love present in his heart. It's like the cold that Comes when there is no heat or the darkness that comes when there is no light."

The professor sat down.

The young man's name--- Albert Einstein

Genius! What is your definition of Genius! Well you might say people like Einstein are genius or a top scorer is a genius. Then you are not wrong but you are not correct as well. Every one of us is a born Genius. But that Genius is made to slumber in darkness by social conditioning and beliefs. Genius or for your simplicity a top scorer carry an attitude and different approach and thinking which if you master, you will end up being one of them.

If you want to be an engineer you don't start rediscovering all fundamental principles of physics which has already been discovered on your own rather you learn it from an Engineer. Correct me if I'm wrong. Same rule applies here. So let's follow the footstep of a top scorer .

If you follow the step by step strategies given in this book and apply it consistently and diligently, I promise you by the time you finish reading this book, there will be marked improvement in your performance and you would awaken the sleeping genius within you. Best of Luck.

WARNING

If you read further and apply these concepts consistently, You would awaken the Genius within You.

<u>Why Learning is essential?</u>

Insanity: doing the same thing over and over again and expecting different results.

-- AlbertEinstein

Why Learning is essential?

Why learning is essential? Hmm it's like asking why breathing is important. Well all human beings are born learners. If you don't believe me then tell me how did you learn to speak your mother tongue so fluently without attending any classes? Well you are correct your parents taught you but who was learning unconsciously? You were, isn't it? Infact Scientific evidences prove that we all were learning unconsciously even before our birth in our mother's womb. We started learning unconsciously every second, every minute, every day from someone but every time after our birth and we are still in the process of learning. You see, Learning never stops. It probably stops the moment we inhale our last breath on this mother Earth. I said probably because who knows we still might be learning after our death as many spiritual Gurus say there is a life after death. We learn from our parents, our friends, a stranger and often from our experiences. We learn from material things. All Scientist learn from nature by observing natural phenomenon. Newton learnt that there is a force which we call Gravitational force which is attracting each and every particle on this Earth by just observing the apple which fell from a tree.

Now today we are in the fastest changing, the most unpredictable and the most unstable time in human history. Yes, we are in the so called Information and communication age. Today information exchange happens in the flick of a second. Just press a button and there is a downpour of loads of information at your desktop. There is a nuclear explosion of information. We have moved from manpower to mind power. Today a person can becomes multi millionaire in couple of hours without any investment of money or raw material by participating in reality shows like K.B.C. The only required investment today is time and brain power.

Today there is no stability in the sense that there has never been stability in the Government, no stability in the stock market. In fact there is no stability in the job as well. You might get into some company today but tomorrow you might be fired without any notice.

Today newly developed software gets outdated within the period of three months. Today an educated and qualified individual is worried about how to stay alive for months and years ahead.

Everyday there is a new invention, new discovery. Today technology changes with unbelievable speed. We have already seen the transition of audio cassettes to CD (compact disc) to usb drives to cloud.

Today Companies before employing look out for something called as Learn ability Index i.e. how fast the individual can learn new information and gets adapted to the needs of the company. If your Learn-ability index is high then you will be on the fast trek to the highest position in the company. But if your Learn-ability index is low then you are either glued to the same position or probably might be fired because of inertia in your performance.

Today, you as a student have an advantage over your seniors as you are exposed to latest state of art facilities i.e. latest technology thereby making you more competent. That means by the same token your juniors will be more competent than you. You never know what is there in the future so it's better to be prepared in advance by learning essential skills as time goes on.

All the people today fall in one of the three categories based on Learn-ability index:

1) Ignorant
2) So called Learned
3) Enlightened

Ignorant people are people with low or almost zero Learn-ability index who usually say,' what happened'.

So called Learned are people with average Learn-ability index who watch things happening.

Enlightened people are people with high Learn-ability index who make things happen

Now to which category do you belong? Statistically only 10% of the students belong to Enlightened Group and that is the reason why you will find only 10% of the students are highly successful. The only one extra thing these 10% students have which other group of students lack is the ability to learn and re-learn and keep on learning new things rapidly and using it in their profession to get high degree of accomplishments.

The only thing today which will help you to be successful and competent is by Learning to Learn. It is this ability which will keep you updated with the new information there by making you more successful in the months and years ahead.

Today the time is so ruthless that it does not give you time to settle down as the technology keeps on changing. Learning to learn is an essential skill which will take care of such turbulent times as you will be already aware and prepared for such time using the ability of Learning.

Change is inevitable. Nothing remains stagnant. Only dead fish go with the flow. Change is the law of nature. If you are not moving ahead chances are you are moving behind. Nobody wants to be at the same place in life. Everybody wants progress and that too rapidly. Today a fresh batch of qualified individual is ready to work at far less salary with more efficiency than what you are earning for competition.

So if you want to improve your learn-ability index then do read the chapters ahead.

Best of Luck for your future.

Why do we need Exam?

Why do we need Exams?

This is a question that is therein some corner of the mind of most students. Think about it, why do we need exam?.Well let us become creative and visualize that God has heard your plea and he has granted your wish, "There won't be any exams".

Control yourself, I know you want to jump and scream at the top of your voice that your most dreaded fear is no longer there. Let's continue our imagination.

Well let's say you wanted to become an Engineer and in the absence of exams it's pretty easy to become anything you desire. Let's say you cleared your 12th STD without giving exams and the day has arrived for the admission in your favorite Engineering College you always dreamt about.

Since any one can apply for engineering, online admission is full before you get a chance. Well that is bound to happen as there are no exams so don't complain now.

When you reach home disappointed you found that your friend who was worst than you in studies and never ever read a single page of any book has invited you for a party celebrating the event of getting admission in the same Engineering college. How does it feel?

Worst than that imagine staying in a building constructed by your same friend or imagine getting operated by a doctor who like your friend never studied medicine and surgery in the absence of exams. Don't you think that not only yours but everybody's life will be a chaos theory? Finally you would ask God again to revert back the wish you asked for, isn't it?

Ask a top scorer about exams and you will be surprised by his answer. For a top scorer, exam is a pathway to success. Exams are not meant to torture you. Exam helps you to succeed by revealing your mistakes and gives you signals to rectify it. Exams help you to reach your best potential by showing you your weak areas. Exams points out your strength and weakness. Exams teaches you practical lessons of life of how to develop your goals and remain focus oriented towards your goals which only a genius understand and hence success lies at his feet. Exam is your friend who guides your carrier. For top scorer Exam is a tool to reveal himself to the entire world. Exam is like a Coach training your mind to achieve best in your life. Remember even diamond is formed under adverse pressure and temperature. Even Survival of human species has been test of nature according to Darwin, a great biologist.

Remember it's not the exam which is your fear, its the Fear itself which is the cause of the problem. Fear shuts all your doors of your mind causing you to go blank in your exam, when you see the test papers. Fear creates stress and blocks you to reach your full potential. Fear is the root cause of your under performance in your exams.

And the good news is Fear is just a thought in your mind causing you to imagine negative things which becomes your ultimate reality. Think about it!

Change your thought about exams and your fear will cease to exist and your reality will change causing you to perform well. Think about exam as your friend sitting beside you in your exams helping you to write the answers and your fear of exams will go away. It is this thought about exams makes an average student atop performer. It's more of mental game than physical hard work which makes a student genius.

In the further chapters I would be discussing few laws of mental game which will awaken the genius within you. So keep on reading and more than that don't try to analyze too much because sometimes analysis does not allow you to think out of box. I would advise you, being a coach of you that apply whatever is said in this book and then introspect..

Hypnosis Of belief

Someone's opinion need not become your reality!

Before we move on to the next chapter I want you to answer the following questions?

1.Can you think of getting 96% this academic year? Ans[Yes / No]

_____

2.Can you get 90%?

Ans_____

_____

_____

In my seminars, when I ask questionno.1, the result is very surprising, seldom any one raises hand. Facial expressions of most students are very sadistic after hearing this question from me. One common answer is 'No' and my answer to that is "and you never got 96% in your entire academic carrier". I will explain that in a moment. There is a law which governs each of us and that law is 'Law of Belief' and it says whatever you believe with conviction, will becomes your reality. Many students believe with conviction that it's not possible for them to score 96% and according to the Law of Belief this belief manifest into reality that they are never able to score 96% in their entire academic carrier unless they chose to change their belief. Think about it.
Ok go through question 1 again. I just asked you to think of getting 96%. I never asked you to get 96%. The problem is many students never think of getting96% so how would they manifest it. What about you?

Now when I ask question #2then many students share a common answer 'I will try'. I asked the same question to a top scorer and the answer was 'I must get minimum 90%'.Whatwas your answer?

My primary aim was to find out what makes a student score less percentage and the other good percentage even though they study the same stuff, encounter the same question and probably go to same tuition. What is the fundamental belief of a top scorer? What role does belief play in achieving success?

What I found is winning is more of Mental game and our beliefs play central role in determining our attitude and thoughts. Change a belief and your reality will change that's it. This chapter is completely devoted to understanding beliefs. After you read this chapter once which starts from next page, I want you take inventory of your beliefs and find out what is stopping you in getting astounding results not only in your academic carrier but in every field of your life.

Hypnosis Of belief

One day, a boy went to the circus with his father and saw a huge elephant tied to a tiny stake with a rope.

"Daddy", asked the boy, "This Elephant is so big and strong and the stake is so small and short, he could set himself free just by taking two steps to the side. Why doesn't he do it?"
And his father said, "My son, when this elephant was very small, just a baby, he did try to break away from this stake, but he wasn't strong enough. He tried and tried for months, until he finally gave up, believing that it is impossible to break free. Now, he doesn't try anymore, because he doesn't believe it's possible. The mighty Elephant has been hypnotized by his own limiting belief.
We are the same, my dear friends. Many things happen to us at childhood, which we try to change, but then stop trying. Many of us are still tied with ropes to tiny stakes, just like this big elephant". We are hypnotized by our own beliefs.
There is a festival of thanks giving in South India called 'Thaipusam'. People pierce long slender rods through their cheeks, pierce hooks on their back and other body parts. The surprising fact is they don't feel pain and they don't even bleed. They are in complete trance like state as they are completely hypnotized by their religious belief. Such is the power of belief that it can stop bleeding even if long slender rod has been pierced through the body.
Upto 1954 it was believed that the human body could simply not run a mile in under 4 minutes. That was the year Roger Bannister shattered that belief, by running a mile in under 4 minutes. Interestingly, Roger said that it was in his mind that he really made the achievement– he ran the 4-minute mile so many times in his imagination that he made it a total belief and then an achievement. Perhaps more interesting, Within the following 12 months 37 other runners had broken the 4 minute mile, and within a further 12 months another 300 hundred had followed suit.

What had changed in such a short period to time to allow this to happen? The simple answer is beliefs. And from deeply held beliefs flowed achievements. So because of a globally held belief that it could not be done, it wasn't. But when Roger challenged and disproved that belief, other people challenged their beliefs and believed it could be done, and it was. Thus the power of belief system is demonstrated.

Hypnosis of belief is also demonstrated from the following example.

1) Yale professor and author Dr. Bernie Siegel has carried out research into people suffering from Multiple Personality Disorders. This disorder is such that the sufferers believe that they are a totally different person at different times. In recorded cases, such was the potency of these beliefs that there is documented evidence of eye colour changing literally from black to blue, physical marks disappearing and diabetes coming and going with each personality

2) At a football game in Los Angeles, it seems that a small number of people experienced what looked like the symptoms of food poisoning. Each of them told the doctor on call that they had consumed a drink from a vending machine. An announcement was made to the crowd to the effect that they should not purchase from the machine until further notice, due to the possibility of food poisoning. What followed was described as pandemonium as people retched &vomited and ambulances were busy all day bringing sick people to hospital. Everything suddenly calmed down when it was discovered that the drink had nothing at all to do with the sickness. It was later reported that many of those who got sick had never even had a drink.
 What is a belief and from where do they come from?
A belief is a collection of thoughts or ideas that you accept as true. "Once accepted, our beliefs become unquestioned commands to our nervous systems, and they have the power to expand or destroy the possibilities of our Present and Future." says Anthony Robbins

For example, we have a belief about our parents, our friends, our teachers, our school, our college, our country, and our enemies and so on. We have a belief about our self. Once you have a belief, you are hypnotized by this belief. You are under the magical spell of this belief which at times becomes difficult to break. Beliefs keep on communicating with us through what I call it "internal dialogues". Many students have a belief about particular subject say Maths or Science. You may find these subjects interesting or boring depending upon the experiences you would have experienced in your childhood. Some of you would have scored fewer marks in Maths or Science in your earlier standards. Your parent and teachers told you that you are weak in Math or Science. Many of your friends might have scored less marks or might have flunked, which makes your negative beliefs about these subjects even stronger and even you start finding difficult to score in these subjects. Instead of questioning yourself why you got less marks?, you start believing that these subjects is not your cup of tea and it gets registered in your mind as a belief which ultimately becomes your reality.

After reading some of the literature on beliefs, I have began to understand that at birth each of us is a blank canvas onto which is painted all the beliefs of those in our world. These people are mostly our parents, our siblings and teachers in the early days. But in those early days we accept the beliefs we are given, as we have nothing to match them against, we have no other reference points. So we unquestioningly accept the beliefs our parents teach us.

How the belief is finally held or changed is probably down to many issues

Including the your self-esteem and your relationship with your parents, but in any case a choice has to be made, and this is the nature of belief– they are beliefs until they are challenged, and at that point it is the strength of the challenge that determines if belief turns to disbelief.

The human mind works in such a way that it seeks out confirmation of its beliefs. Infact it seeks references and supports to hold them in place. Indeed, the mind will ensure that we act and react in such a way as to prove our beliefs. We will seek out and find evidence to prove our beliefs. In effect, our beliefs will become a self-fulfilling prophecy, making real what we believe to be true. If we believe that few subjects like Maths/ Science /Languages are difficult to score, then we will unconsciously seek information to support this belief! And will we find it? Of course we will, and if not we will create a situation where we will find scoring in these subjects are really difficult!

Humans unconsciously carry out three types of information filtering, all the time. We Generalize Delete and Distort information. Each of these helps us survive and function effectively.

But we will use the same processes to support our beliefs! We will generalise that all Maths/Science subject is difficult because we had an experience of scoring bad marks in Math/Science Exam. To support this we will delete any information that might challenge this i.e. only focus on the bad points. And we will then distort any evidence that we cannot delete i.e. well the paper looks easy but I know I won't be able to solve it. So beliefs are a feeling of certainty about something. It is useful to use a Metaphor of a table to think about this. The belief is the tabletop, and the legs supporting the tabletop are the proof, rationalization or justification for that belief - the legs are the references we seek and store to hold up the belief.

If I hold a belief that I am intelligent, then that is my tabletop. Let's say that I got this belief from my parents, and that they reinforced it regularly,

No matter what I did. In my formative years this belief is taken on board without question, as I have no other references. These are strong legs under this table. Then I begin to play outside and an older child tells me that I am stupid. And all the other kids laugh at this! For the first time in my young and secure life my belief in my intelligence is under threat– one of these support legs is being sawed down. My feeling of certainty is being eroded.

Now different children will react to such a situation in different ways, but if the belief is to be held strongly then the leg under attack needs to be mended, and quickly. And from that moment on, the belief will be searching for new references from which to build support legs, to keep the belief alive. If in that moment of pain, the leg was actually broken from under the table, then it may be that this belief will never be rebuilt again.

Therefore, it seems that these beliefs that can cause such success or such misery are actually subject to modification, sometimes in an instant. This is a crucial understanding in the study of human relations.

It is useful to divide beliefs into 3 categories or levels: opinions, beliefs and convictions. One can see that inherent in the wording is the idea of the strength of the belief, or, the strength of the feeling of certainty, that a person holds about a particular issue. To continue the metaphor from above, a belief becomes one of the three categories depending on the quantity or strength of the references that are supporting it i.e. the strength of the legs under the table.

If we get a belief from someone who we really look upto, admire and respect then it can hold the strength of a conviction –I might hurt or even kill someone to defend this belief. On the other hand, an opinion has more shaky legs under the table, and it is likely that I could be swayed quite easily by being shown some minor new references.

Often people will hold onto beliefs because of the pain / pleasure principle. This principle holds that we will do anything to avoid pain and gain pleasure, and is worth thinking about in relation to the understanding of belief systems. In this model, our belief systems are acting as a type of guidance mechanism, keeping us moving away from pain and moving towards pleasure.

What might happen when a student holds a belief that is the opposite to that of the Teacher?

Without a firm understanding of the nature of belief systems, this student -teacher relationship cannot function to the highest level of efficiency. That is there as on why even if the teacher, the school, the college might be the best but the student may not be able to score good percentage.

As I am writing this book a student of mine to whom I asked to give test on Science and had given 1 weeks time approached me and said "Sir,

Please give me more time as it's impossible for me to learn 5 chapters in 7 days". I asked him " How many days are left?"Hesaid,"6daysare left". I told him, "How can you predict with certainty that you won't be able to study on the 2nd day with 6 days in hand even before trying it? He said , "I know and I have a strong feeling that I won't be able to study." I told him that you have been hypnotized by yourself limiting belief and it's yourself limiting belief talking to you in your mind that it is impossible for you to study in 7 days and that is the reason why your performance has always been average.

Self limiting belief makes you work in your comfortable zone. When something is out of your comfortable zone west art getting frustrated and you start finding ways to run back to your comfortable zone and that is the reason why you are heart is trying to convince you to give you more time. Remember in Boards you would be having papers practically speaking every alternate day with 1 or 2 day gap and you have to learn entire textbook and students do it without any complain. And if you really want to perform well then start questioning your belief that "Why it is impossible for me to complete the studying task in 7 days?" Many students do it then why can't I? What is that one thing which is stopping me? I will do it. I have to do it. I must do it in 7 days and I know that Iam quite capable of doing things. After what I said this student was astonished and he went back saying "Sir, I will finish it in 7 days". On the 7thdayI asked him, how many chapters did you finish? He said, Sir I was able to finish almost 8 chapters instead of 5.

And if you are thinking that it's impossible to study 8 chapters in 7 days then you have a self limiting belief. Remember yourself limiting belief will always make you do things in which you are very comfortable i.e. 'your comfortable zone'. Genius always work out of there comfortable zone and that is the reason why they are so successful.

Your success in life and your ability to realize your dreams depend upon your ability to conquer your self limiting beliefs. Self limiting beliefs are the single biggest obstacle in keeping your dreams alive and yet so few people really understand the real dangers their beliefs present to them. Ignore your self limiting beliefs and all your dreams will materialize.

How do I know whether a Belief is right or wrong?

Beliefs are neither right nor wrong. There are two types of viz; self limiting or Empowering. The simple way to find out whether a belief is self limiting or empowering is to look at your life. Like roadmaps they determine your path to success. If you have a self limiting belief you will be travelling on a road which never leads to your ultimate destination. Your self limiting belief will create roads in your mind which will be full of obstacles, ups and downs and finally it will lead you to dead end of the road.

Empowering beliefs are like high ways which runs directly to your ultimate goal in life. Empowering beliefs creates an imaginary smooth flyover on a road full of obstacles which goes unnoticed.

What would you do if you were in Edison's place if you failed 1500 times to invent a bulb? Well most of you will quit the 2nd time you failed or even worst the first time.

I'm sure you're asking yourself "Well, does it mean we have to try again and again? When do we learn that certain things are simply impossible and shift our energy to other things?" The answer to that is

"Never! As long as something is important to you, it's possible and you should try to get it again and again". Remember even impossible says that I'm possible.

You see, Thomas Edison tried 1,500 different types of wire to use on the light bulb. 1,500! Do you understand that if Edison thought like us, we would never have light? In a sense, if we don't think like Edison, we stay in the dark.

If you scored less marks in some subject then instead of thinking that you are weak in that subject you should try to find out the reasons of getting less marks and try to rectify it. Now there could be various reasons. May be you didn't study or probably you didn't understand the stuff on the first hand or you knew it but you forgot the moment you saw the question etc. If a top scorer gets fewer marks he or she immediately springs into action and finds out what went wrong and immediately sits down rectifying it. It is this attitude which makes an average student a top scorer.

Now let's take an inventory of your beliefs about different subjects and find out for yourself whether your belief is self limiting or empowering. If it is self limiting start doubting your belief by asking questions starting with "Why" and your self limiting belief will cease to exist. But then after breaking the hypnotic spell of your self limiting belief you need to replace it with an empowering belief starting with "I must" and "I can". The reason is if your negative belief is not replaced by positive ones then the latter will re-emerge again. That is nature's way as even air tries to occupy a vacuum space.

Belief Analysis Sheet

1.Write the name of the subjects which you find difficult?
Your answer: _____

_____

2.If difficult then why?
Your answer: _____

_____

3.Do you think you can score full marks in these subjects ?If 'No' then why?
Your answer: _____

_____

4.Do you practice theorems, diagrams, chemical equation and numerical problems at least thrice a week? If Not then why?
Your answer: _____

_____

5.Do you think the reasons for 'No' in the above answer puts you into your comfortable zone no matter how genuine your reasons might be?
Your answer: _____

_____

6.If you are studying the same stuff and answering the same questions as top scorer does then why do you get less marks and who is stopping you?
Your answer: _____

_____

Make a photo copy of this sheet and answer the same questions for other subjects to find out your self limiting belief.

Procrastination- How to use it effectively

"Procrastination is a game in which you always end up screwing yourself."

-- Sunil Sharma

Procrastination-How to use it effectively ?

"Procrastination is the art of keeping up with yesterday."
-- Don Marquis

A Story of Procrastination
8:31 am. Its eight thirty-one, and I've got nothing. I had four weeks time to study for the coming exam and most importantly for my most dreaded paper Science. Iam supposed to write a test todayat11.30 am on Science and my mind has gone completely blank with a sensation of Gnats swooping around my neck as my pen furiously dances on the paper.
Two hours. Two hours are left to write the paper. Two fleeting hours counting down to judgment day. I had four weeks to study Science but here Iam to tell a story, my story, a story of procrastination. People were crowding around me, not knowing they were distracting me in the last four weeks. My mind is a moth, people are the flame. I fly hopelessly towards them like how moths fly towards flame.
A gust of sudden wind rustles my Science text pages, and I look down. Eight forty-four. I've lost precious time! How can I overcome these distractions? Voices endlessly clamouring my mind. The worst thing is, they keep coming...my friends, my relatives and they're everywhere. The doors fling open and they rush out of the cafeteria, a sudden storm flooding my study space like bugs, like caterpillars. They are caterpillars that eat and eat, devouring my precious time. My time precious time is disappearing, leaving me alone as a frustrated and stressed individual with chemical equations jumping all over my head! All because of the caterpillars i.e. my friends, internet surfing, pc-games, X- box etc.
Suddenly the clock bell rung. My veins contract. My heart stops beating for only a second, but it stops. My hands begin to shake uncontrollably. Now 52 minutes are left! I have52minutes to write Science paper and my mind has been attacked by funny chemical names and never ending list

of diagrams, extraction process, diseases and bla bla things not even god would have studied. I stand and started walking towards my school.

My walk quickens to a sprint. I'm running through the hall sand I don't care what they think because they don't know me. They don't know my situation. They never could... could they? Have these stressful feelings of frustration and shame ever filled their veins? Has aggravation and disappointment ever pumped through their hearts? Have I beena caterpillar?

Ouch!!! Wrist cramp! Is this karma for all the years that I've been the distraction? Well, the tables have turned all right! Has the distraction become the distracted?

In this sudden epiphany, I arrive at class. Students shuffle around their desks, but the room quickly falls silent. My memory begins to return and re-circulate, safely lodging the wretched caterpillars in their cocoons. Chemical Equations are sprouting in my brain. They are growing and I love it.

I love it, but wait... These chemical equations have been tainted by stories filled with laughing, gossip, food, internet surfing, chatting, PC games etc. The answers to every question in the paper have changed in my head to movies, music, internet, sports, mailing and chatting. Worst of all, the paper has become a Villain. How can I write about something I hate? My memory for science and similarly for other subjects has been ruined. They're tainted and useless to me.

The bell rings. The cocoons are hatching and turning the caterpillars into butterflies. Butterflies that want to stay and live in my stomach, swirling and twirling around inside me. They fill me up. They make me want to vomit, vomit out all of these worthless ideas, and my feelings of shame and frustration.

As I approach the door, I can't hold them in any longer. I feel the butterflies escaping through every orifice of my body. My pores pour out sweat. My veins throb. My mouth spits out words, trying to explain everything I've gone through. My dead cat. My participation in extra-curricular ideas. My extreme load of classes.

I want to speak, to say anything, but nothing comes. Something. Anything. They're all excuses anyway, excuses that don't help but delay the inevitability that at the end of this 52-minute class I have a paper due, a paper with metaphors, similes ,alliteration, brush strokes, and most importantly with my voice. My voice tells my story,a story of procrastination. All I have left are my poisoned ideas strung together into a story, my story, a story of procrastination.

So does the story coincide's with your story as well?

The dictionary meaning of Procrastination is to put off doing something, especially out of habitual carelessness or laziness and a Procrastinator is someone who postpones work especially out of laziness or habitual carelessness. It's a very surprising fact that every one of us is a procrastinator at some point of our life.
It's pretty normal to be a procrastinator. The only difference between a Genius and you is only one thing a Genius procrastinates non important things whereas you procrastinate important things. Think about it.
The most amazing fact is a procrastinator already knows that he is procrastinating things but still he procrastinates. The main question is why we procrastinate?

The answer is simple; we procrastinate because:-
•   Lack of clear goals
•   Lack of time management and stress management skills

•   Either over confident or low self confident
•   Lack of Self Discipline
•   Unaware of Self strength and weakness
•   No understanding of the subject
•   When we know we will have to work outside our comfortable zone.
We procrastinate because somewhere deep down inside us we feel pain leaving our comfortable zone. We have unconsciously linked feeling of

pleasure in remaining affix to our comfortable zone and feeling of pain to an uncomfortable zone.

Studying causes to come out of your comfortable zone which is a pain while playing sports or PC Games or surfing internet is pleasurable instead of studying. So you say to yourself Okay, let me enjoy other things first and after that I will finish my studying work. The moment you finish your never ending sports or internet surfing you realize that its time to take rest which is more pleasurable and the studying work is postponed to next day. Again as human beings are creatures of beliefs and habit you follow the same routine even on the next day. Thus the work is postponed indefinitely unless a day comes when there is no chance of postponing. You get frustrated, anxiety and stress builds upon you and somehow under pressure you finish the work with 0.1% performance.

If you are a kind of person who loves to work under pressure or major chunk of work get completed on the last day or you study a day before exam then you are a procrastinator. Nothing wrong in it but your true best does not come out in this way.

All of us have heard the fable of The Ant and the Grasshopper; we saw how the grasshopper put off stocking up food for winter and suffered much later. Here, the Grasshopper highlighted again this procrastinate behaviour that is so common among humans.

Many people claim that they never procrastinate, yet the tell-tale signs indicate otherwise. They may turn up late for school or tuitions because they leave their home late and blame the delay on the slow elevators traffic etc. They do their home work at the last minute or only when they receive reminders. They start studying a day before or a week before exam.

Amazingly, procrastinators can yield results just as good as non-procrastinators. Kids in school can be playing their PSP or Xbox games up till a month before the major exams. That is when they start to flip their books and begin their revision. The learning curve is so steep that within a month, they are at their peak form and pass their exams with flying colours. They burn midnight oil, manage to boost their adrenaline rush, and are able to deliver outstanding work right on time.

These people are not lazy. Their strategy to running a1500m race is to enjoy a slow comfortable pace throughout and sprinting the last 400m stretch upon hearing the bell. A long period of slow or non-activity followed by a short burst of hyperactivity.

There are of course the procrastinators who do not even deliver results. They sit on things for a long time, hoping that they will someday disappear. This is the type of motivational problem that is most worrying. We often hear the myth that it has to do with genes, a like-father-like-son syndrome.

We can control or even overcome our procrastination problem and here are some pointers on how we can do that:-

Relate pleasure in completing the work on time and relate pain in postponing the work

Now habit
Develop a habit of doing it now.

Break it down
If you are not doing the task because it is too huge and onerous, break it into smaller and manageable parts. It is easier to see immediate success in small tasks and this helps motivate you to do the next task.

Set priorities
Set your priorities right. Not everything is of a high priority. Do what is urgent rather than do only what is convenient. Procrastinate non urgent and non important things like chatting, surfing, playing games etc.

Minimize distractions
Minimize or remove distractions – switch off the TV or cell phone, close the door, draw the blinds, adjust the lighting, do not read emails. If you are prone to falling asleep on a comfy chair, switch to a hard stool. Concentrate on getting the job done.

Avoid Time eaters

Normally, it happens many a time that while studying, your friends and relative may intrude into your study place. The sad story is you cannot avoid it and research shows on average they consume17 minutes of your precious time. The best thing what you can do is the moment somebody intrudes your study space stand up and walk along with him towards your door and try to finish your conversation quickly. This is in chatting. Don't keep extra chair in your study room and even if it is there always keep it piled with either books or your stinking socks. Or else you can tell them politely that this is your study hour and you will call them up the moment you finish your work.

Clean desk

Start with having a clean environment. Tidy up the mess on your desktop or in office; put everything in neat order.

Do it for yourself

Sometimes you may dislike the person who handed you the task and choose to drag your feet. Do not see yourself as doing the job for your boss or your parents; do it for yourself. You have a reputation to keep, a personal challenge to meet. Completing the job is an accomplishment added to your belt; you did it, not them.

Set goals

Be realistic about your goals. Do not expect too much in yourself by setting unattainable goals. Too much of a perfectionist and nothing will be done.

Think of consequences

What if the job is not done? Think of the consequences. Will you still have to do it? Will you or somebody close to you be penalized? Often, knowing that you will have to eventually do the job makes you want to dispose of it sooner than later.

Reward yourself

Treat yourself to some rewards whenever a task, small or big, is completed. Do something to make you feel good and remind yourself of the task you have accomplished.

Get started

However contradictory this sounds, try to get started on something. If you are doing a written assignment, write whatever that comes into your mind. Once the thoughts are on paper, it is easier to editor re-write. There is seldom a right time or right mood to do things, so take a first step and see where it leads you.

<u>Exam Fear</u>

Exam Fear

This is one fear to which many of you fear a lot. Few students get something called as Exam sickness. Hands and feet go cold and mind goes blank. You start perspiring and get sudden uneasiness in your stomach and felt like running away and hiding somewhere or something should happen so hat exam gets postponed. If you have felt any of the symptoms above mentioned then you have what we call EXAM FEAR. Our brain is an amazing organ. It can remember everything and interpret them well, more than a computer. Its working nature seems to be a mystery, i.e., it is thought of or get the thing one wishes to forget, and it is difficult to remember the thing one wishes to remember and your bad luck that your brain forgets at very crucial time of exam. Anyhow, for all learners, the brain's cooperation is very much essential. When one gets tensed or is fearful, one can often go blank as if the condition/situation
/circumstance had formatted their brain.
March has always been dreaded season or a tension period for all students due to exam fear. Many of you sacrifice TV, outings, tours, sleep, pc games etc., atleast for the sake of getting clear in your exam. Many of you find yourself losing concentration and will often become frustrated, irritated and worried causing exam fear. On top of that, your parents would often complain that you are studying well but not scoring well. At this juncture rather than blaming you should go for analysis of the cause to rectify/ treat it
One's incompetence and ignorance usually debar them from their activities unless good luck plays a major role. Many student opt for several health drinks or product which according to them will increase their memory and IQ Level. Actually speaking, it is difficult to prove the gain of IQ, since it needs not only brain boosters but also one's interest in learning, ability, tendency to concentrate, good teaching, favourable circumstances, etc. Here brain needs more exercises than just a brain booster - Learning and recalling –just like contraction and relaxation of

muscles as we do for our physique. Squeezing the brain during childhood is good for one's life in future. Here one needs to remember the old proverb

I hear –I forget
I see – I remember
I do –I understand and will never forget
Unwanted tension can precipitate exam fear.
Causes– are usually numerous, but the common causes are:

- Lack of memory or forgetfulness i.e. no memory training.
- Fear of punishments from parents /teachers.
- Low Self Confidence.
- Lack of Goal planning skills.
- Lack of time management and Stress management skills.
- Procrastination-putting off things for tomorrow what can be done today.
- Low self esteem.
- Poor study strategies
- Improper learning i.e. studying not in depth
- Inattentive/distracted mind
- Health problems

Exam fear can cause a variety of symptoms. The common symptoms are:

- Fear and sweat, and some others would sink and faint in addition.
- Some others get tremors, nervousness; sometimes they find it difficult to control passing of urine and stools.
- Feeling blank or vagueness before exam
- Difficulty in concentrating and studying while preparing for exams
- Fear to appear for exams
- Getting tensed on seeing difficult questions
- Difficulty in expressing / presentation even for known answers due to fear or inferiority complex

- Confusion and hopelessness
- Sweating and racing heart
- Dizziness due to sleepless study
- Tension and worries

Prevention and management–
- Learn Goal Setting and Time management skills.
- Learn Memory skills to learn and recall answers.
- Learn to take good care of your health during the exam period or otherwise every effort taken in studying will go in vain. Take plenty of vegetables, dairy products, cereals, pulses, nuts, etc. Also, be aware that it is not worth just supplementing without any exercises, i.e., only an active body keeps an energetic brain.
- Never overload your stomach, since it may induce sleep.
- Learn to increase your concentration.
- Keep everything in memory in inter-relationship using mind map
- Revise in the mornings (early morning is the best time, since brain will be more active after a good sleep)
- Prepare for exams right from the beginning and well in advance
- Have confidence that you have learnt everything, you will remember everything, you will present everything and finally you will achieve your goal.
- Understand the question in depth, answer aptly in a cool manner, without any tension
- Don't Study continuously (day and night) – relax often to re-charge your brain
- Cold beverages/things generally should be avoided so that you don't get unnecessary cold and fever during exam period causing Stress and worries
- Never ever Underestimate yourself
- Start studying as soon as teacher teaches the chapter never procrastinate
- Learn self discipline

- Learn to organize yourself i.e. keep your notes and assignment complete and keep it at proper place.
- Don't Discuss new things or unknown things before entering the exam hall
- Don't Get tensed by the speed of others in writing and collecting additional sheets
- Don't Feel running out of time - relax, set mind to proceed in good speed and spirit till the end of time
- Don't get blank on seeing tough questions – on those occasions, just skip that question and go with the next known and simple one. In the meantime, your brain will become energetic enough to answer any sort of questions in an easy manner.

If you follow all these good Luck will be always yours.

<u>Self Confidence</u>

"Don't wait until everything is just right. It will never be perfect. There will always be challenges, obstacles and less than perfect conditions. So what. Get started now. With each step you take, you will grow stronger and stronger, more and more skilled, more and more self-confident and more and more successful."

SELF CONFIDENCE

What is Self confidence?

Once upon a time all village people decided to pray for rain. On the day of prayer all people gathered and only one boy came with an umbrella that's self confidence...

Self Confidence is feeling inside you that YOU CAN and low Self Confidence is a feeling inside you that YOU CAN'T and this world respects, admire, listen and follow a person with high self confidence. People with high self confidence have already reached half the way to success. Well nobody wants to follow, listen or admire a person who is not confident about what he is speaking about and I'm sure even you won't? Isn't it?

There is a thin line of difference between Self Confidence and Over Confidence. A person with a feeling that he/she can is a Self Confident person whereas a person with a feeling that Only he / She can is an over confident and egoistic person.

According to Urban dictionary a Person is Over-Confident who declares his victory without assessing his capabilities or the final result or situations.

E.g. Congress party in India was over-confident of its winning in 2014 Lok-Sabha Elections but Mr. Narendra Modi won after so much of criticism.

Your level of self-confidence can show in many ways: Your behaviour, your body language, how you speak, what you say, and so on. Low self-confidence can be self-destructive, and it often manifests itself as negativity. Self-confident people are generally more positive – they believe in themselves and their abilities, and they also believe in the wonders of living life to the full.

So what is your Self Confidence level? Let's analyze it.

Analyze your Self Confidence Level. Go through the low confidence symptoms and put a check mark if you have that symptom.

Signs of low Self Confidence:

1)   Feeling that you are forgetting answers just 1 hour before exam.

2)   Feeling that you won't be able to complete the paper in time.

3)   Not able to Speak and keep your views in front of class.

4)   Your hand and feet shivers and you perspire a lot while giving speech.

5)   You know the answer of a question asked by a teacher in a class but you don't have the courage to raise your hand

6)   Public Speaking is a big No – No.

7)   Someone appreciates you and you feel shy and feel uncomfortable about it.

8)   You always try to run away from being in limelight.

9)   If you see someone laughing at you, you always feel that they are mocking at you.

10)   Feeling that you are useless.

11)   Feeling that others are better than you.

12)   Not able to take decision.
13)   Not able to speak with someone with direct eye contact but looking here and there.

14)   Fear of Criticism and hence avoid taking risk.

15)   Fear of failure and hence avoid taking responsibility.

Now count the number of check mark and analyze for yourself from the table below:

No of Check Mark	Analysis
2	Good Self Confidence
From 3 to5	Average Self Confidence
More than5	Low Self Confidence

Now how to Develop the Self-Confidence You Deserve! Building Self-Confidence. In my experience with successful people, I would say the main factor that separates the successful people from those that are not is that one small word –Self Confidence Synonyms for confidence are faith, belief, trust, reliance, dependence, and self-assurance. I really believe strongly in the idea: 'If you think you can, or you think you can't- You're right!?I don't know anyone who has achieved a high degree of success, be it money, leadership, recognition, or even a great family foundation, that didn't have confidence. It is one of the vital keys to reaching our full potential. How can we gain confidence in our own abilities? What steps can we take every day to build our confidence if we feel it isn't there yet? And how do you build this sense of balanced self-confidence, founded on a firm appreciation of reality?
The bad news is that there's no quick fix, or 5-minute solution.
The good news is that building self-confidence is readily achievable, just as long as you have the focus and determination to carry things through. And what's even better is that the things you'll do will build success – after all, your confidence will come from real, solid achievement. No-one can take this away from you!
Remember a person is not confident because he is not sure about something and this low self confidence arises and takes toll because of lack of clear plan and goals. But what I have seen is people do have goals but then one thing is very common with such people that they do not

have it in the written form which is a tanligible thing which is not same in the case of successful people.

All successful people maintain a list of written goals which they go through every now and then to keep checking whether they are on right track. It's a tangible thing which they can touch it and feel it.

Here are few steps and if you follow each step religiously I promise you will be a new born self confident person. So go ahead…

1. Write out a plan:
'If you fail to plan, you plan to fail? A plan is crucial in any endeavour: football teams have a play book of plans, contractors plan things out before building a home, professional speakers have a plan before they take the stage, teachers use a curriculum.

2. Review your plan frequently:
Remember, remember, remember! It's so easy for us to make the excuse - I forgot to do that. That's why reviewing your plan at least daily can help. Post the plan on your bathroom mirror, tape it to your car dashboard, write it in your planner, do whatever YOU need to do to remind yourself of steps you need to take

3. Tell someone about your plan and ask them to hold you accountable:
It's far too easy to quit and give up on yourself when things don't seem to go as easy as you think they should. That's why it's good to have someone there to help you through and encourage you to stick to it.

4. Record your progress:
'Small Success leads to Big Success!? I know, many of you probably hear this too much. However, those that record their progress really seem to be getting to levels that they never imagined were possible. It can be so rewarding to read back over the steps you've taken to get where you are, even if they are very small. It's always the little things we do every day which help us get where we want to go.

5. Revise your plan from time to time:

Don't be afraid to make adjustments. Change your strategy, especially if what you are doing isn't taking you where you want to go.

6. Look at what you've already achieved:

Think about your life so far, and list the ten best things you've achieved in an "Achievement Log." Perhaps you came top in an important test or exam. Put these into a smartly formatted document, which you can look at often. And then spend a few minutes each week enjoying the success you've already had!

7. Think about your strengths:

Next, use a technique like SWOT Analysis to take a look at who and where you are. Fill up the SWOT analysis sheet at the end of the chapter and then continue reading from here. Looking at your Achievement Log, and reflecting on your recent life, think about what your friends would consider to be your strengths and weaknesses. From these, think about the opportunities and threats you face. Make sure that you enjoy a few minutes reflecting on your strengths!

8. Think about what's important to you and where you want to go:

Next, think about the things that are really important to you, and what you want to achieve with your life. Setting and achieving goals is a key part of this, and real self-confidence comes from this. Goal setting is the process you use to set yourself targets, and measure your successful hitting of those targets. Set goals that exploit your strengths, minimize your weaknesses, realize your opportunities, and control the threats you face.

9. Start managing your mind:

At this stage, you need to start managing your mind. Learn to pick up and defeat the negative self-talks which can destroy your confidence. Read the chapter hypnosis of belief. And learn how to use visualization technique to create strong mental images of what you'll feel and experience as you achieve your major goals –there's something about doing this that makes even major goals seem achievable!

10. And then commit yourself to success!
The final part of preparing for the journey is to make a clear and unequivocal promise to yourself that you are absolutely committed to your journey, and that you will do all in your power to achieve it. If as you're doing it, you find doubts starting to surface write them down and challenge them calmly and rationally. If they dissolve under scrutiny, that's great. However if they are based on genuine risks, make sure you set additional goals to manage these appropriately. Either way, make that promise!

11. Setting Out
This is where you start, ever so slowly, moving towards your goal. By doing the right things, and starting with small, easy wins, you'll put yourself on the path to success – and build the self-confidence that comes with this.

12. Build the knowledge you need to succeed:
Looking at your goals, identify the skills you'll need to achieve them. And then look at how you can acquire these skills confidently and well. Don't just accept a sketchy, just-good-enough solution –look for a solution that fully equips you to achieve what you want to achieve.

13. Focus on the basics:
When you're starting, don't try to do anything clever or elaborate. And don't reach for perfection –just enjoy doing simple things successfully and well.

14. Set small goals, and achieve them:
Starting with the very small goals you identified get in the habit of setting them, achieving them, and celebrating that achievement. Don't make goals particularly challenging at this stage, just get into the habit of

achieving them and celebrating them. And little by little, start piling up the successes!

15. Accelerating Towards Success
By this stage, you'll feel your self-confidence building and you'll have plenty of success to celebrate!

16.Now's the time to start stretching yourself.
Make the goals a bit bigger, and the challenges a bit tougher. Increase the size of your commitment. And
extend the skills you've proven into new, but closely related arenas.

17. Confidence is about you- enthusiasm is about your subject As long as you are focused on 'being confident', you are the focus of attention. And when it's all about you, it's very easy to get caught up in self-doubt ("Am I really up to this? Will I be able to do it?"). But when you focus on a subject that's important to you- the work you're presenting, the information you want to share, the message you're trying to get across - then chances are you'll find yourself overtaken by enthusiasm. You will be energized, your voice will sound stronger, your hands will start gesturing, and you'll find your whole body moving as you warm to your task. You will lose your self-consciousness and be lost in the work itself, in the words and ideas you want to get across.

18. Confidence is about you(again)- enthusiasm is about others I repeat-when you are trying to be confident, your attention is on yourself. But when you focus on your audience - whether one person, a roomful or a whole stadium - you stop worrying about your own performance. Instead, your attention is on the audience's experience: How are the ideas coming across? How do they look? Engaged? Confused? Intrigued? Have they 'got it' yet? If not, what can you do to help them? What feedback are they giving you? How can you use this to make it easier for them to learn, to enjoy or to see your point of view? How can you get them to share your enthusiasm?

19. Confidence is impressive – enthusiasm is infectious

How many times have you watched a presenter or met someone and been impressed with their confident manner – but without really warming to them? Confidence can be impressive, but beware the kind of impression you are leaving. Enthusiasm on the other hand, is highly infectious. Think of a time when you heard someone talk about a subject you had previously no interest in, but they were so enthusiastic about it, you could not help being intrigued, even fascinated. There is something contagious about the body language of enthusiasm - when you see someone talking excitedly, smiling, gesturing, full of energy and keen to share what they know, you can't help responding. It is as though at some level we look at an enthusiastic person and think "That looks good, that looks fun" and can't resist the urge to join in.

20. Confidence is certain- enthusiasm is creative

You can feel confident when you know what you are doing, and are sure you can do it well. There are lots of times and places for this kind of confidence, but too much certainty can be stifling. With enthusiasm, there is always an element of uncertainty, the excitement of not knowing exactly what you are going to say next and looking forward to surprising yourself. That is why scripted speeches are so dull, and why the atmosphere at an improvised show is electric. Accounts of the creative process abound with stories of images, ideas or words 'popping into' someone's mind – and invariably, the subject or medium is one for with the person has huge enthusiasm.

21. Confidence is serious - enthusiasm is fun

When you start talking or thinking about being confident, you are likely to start taking things a bit seriously. When you want to be confident about doing something, it is because you think it is important. And when something is important, it means Bad Things can happen if you get it wrong. Thinking about Bad Things is enough to make anyone serious. But when you're enthusiastic, importance translates into passion- and the whole thing becomes fun. There are few things more enjoyable than talking enthusiastically about something you are passionate about, and feeling others share your enthusiasm. I will climb off the soap-box now. Enthusiasm is one of my enthusiasms. What are yours?

22. Be willing to change and know what will stop you. Become familiar with your negative ego, your inner critics, the art of you that objects to your becoming more, that will sabotage what you're doing. Where will that lead you? What will you get out of pretending to be small? Go looking for that part of you, so that you can anticipate what might stop you and be proactive.

23. Embrace your imperfections
Mistakes and defeats are bound to happen, and it's okay. Be curious about them, grab hold of them. They present you with wonderful opportunities to learn about yourself. Don't let those opportunities slip by. Don't dilute them with judgments about yourself. Instead, what can you learn?

24. Be nervous
Regularly, do something that makes you nervous, that stretches you into more of who you truly are and can be. Don't wait to be on your A-Game.

25. Pursue deep challenges, be restless
Don't dabble. Too much of life awaits. Engage your life passionately. Make a difference Make your life matter Laugh often and have fun

SWOT Analysis

SWOT(Strength, Weakness, Opportunity, Threat) analysis is a useful technique that can be used by a student on a personal level to find Strength and Weakness.

SWOT analysis has been widely used as a problem-solving and goal-planning tool. It can help you to focus on key issues of relevance to the subject in hand. When used in this way it can show us how to take full advantage of your talent and abilities. It can help to uncover new learning opportunities and eliminate perceived threats in the learning environment.

How do I apply SWOT analysis?

You might want to explore ways in which you can personalize learning and develop differentiation in the classroom. Consider this by asking yourself questions in terms of our areas:

Strengths:
What are your personal strengths and their sources available to you?

Weaknesses:
In what areas could you improve?

Opportunities:
What are the opportunities in school that you enjoy? What possibilities can you see for developing your learning?

Threats:
What are the obstacles or barriers that you face? Do they present threats to your learning?

Brainstormtheseideaswithyourself.Itdoesn'tmatterabouttheorderofthe thoughts as it is more important to map your ideas, record them on paper and use this as aspiring board for development.

Once you have got your strengths, weaknesses, opportunities and threats worked out, you can begin to consider if the strengths and opportunities outweigh the weaknesses and threats. They may see that there is an immediate threat that means the idea is not viable. Try to get them to think a little deeper to see if the idea can be changed in some way to minimize this threat.

It is easy to design a simple work sheet for this purpose.

Here are some questions you could explore with yourself:

Strengths

1.   Which subjects you are good at?

Your answer: _____

_____

2.   What do others think you are good at?

Your answer: _____

_____

3.   What do you enjoy studying?

Your answer: _____

_____

4.   What areas you are competent in that are not just subject specific? (Think in wider terms of emotional and social intelligence too.)

Your answer: _____

_____

5.   What subjects do you get good marks in? Are there particular learning styles that I lean towards?

Your answer: _____

Weaknesses

1. Are there any specific subjects, skills or areas that you are weak?
Your answer: _____

_____

2 .Do you have any specific learning difficulties, eg dyslexia?
Your answer: _____

_____

Opportunities

1. How can you use your strengths to overcome your weakness?
Your answer: _____

_____

2. What strategies could you devise or use to appeal to your strengths and compensate for your weaknesses?
Your answer: _____

_____

3. What motivates you?
Your answer: _____

_____

4. Howcould you(or your teacher) make small adjustments to help you learn more effectively?
Your answer: _____

_____

Threats

1.   What makes you feel uncomfortable in class?
Your answer: _____

_____

2.   What hinders you or stops you from learning? What de-
motivates you?
Your answer: _____   _____

_____

Do not use the SWOT tool as fixed and permanent measure-people
change!

Self Image and Self Esteem

"Low self-esteem is like driving through life with your hand-break on."

Self Image and Self Esteem

There are few students who simply don't progress no matter whatever techniques they learn. They have got developed something called 'Inertia' in physics. Their common dialogs are
'No matter whatever I do this subject does not go into my head', 'I'm weak at this subject', 'I always forget in exam', 'Iam not a scholar' etc. In such cases it is not that the technique is a problem. It's the problem of Self Image. It's like running a poor Operating system which consequently makes the computer to hang. With negative self image you cannot succeed in any field of life. Well its rightly said, if you want to succeed you got to install a good operation system i.e. developing a positive self image about yourself.

Positive Self Image is the top secret of a top scorer. Now the next question in your mind must be :

What is self-image?
Self-image is:
- How you perceive yourself.
- The mental picture of how you believe you appear to others.
- How you picture your physical self i.e. your body image
- How you believe others see you physically.
- Your idea(positive or negative, rational or irrational) of how you present yourself to others and how you are subsequently judged by them.
- A personal assessment of your character, personality, skills, abilities, and other attributes.
- A powerful internal mechanism influencing how you feel about yourself.
- An accumulation of scripts you have been given (consciously or otherwise) and have learned well throughout your life.

Surprisingly it may seem that most of the time we always have a distorted image of our self which may not be actually true. It is similar like when you record your voice and then you hear it and you say to yourself with disbelief that 'Oh! Is that my voice? Do I sound like that? It happens because when you hear your own voice while you speak, the sound which reaches to your brain is distorted. Its not your real voice. The real voice is the one which you hear on the recorder. Now it really boils down to whether that distorted image is a healthy image or an unhealthy image.

You might have a negative self image about yourself about you performing in particular subject like Math is not in my genes.

Your self-image can be very different from how the world sees you. Some people who outwardly seem to have it all (intelligence, looks, personal and financial success) may have a bad self-image and hence indulge in drug addiction conversely, others who have had a very difficult life and multiple hardships may have a very positive self-image. Some believe that a person's self-image is defined by events that affect him or her like doing well or not in school, work, or relationships. Others believe that a person's self-image can help shape those events. There is probably some truth to both schools of thought: failing at something can certainly cause one to feel bad about oneself, just as feeling good about oneself can lead to better performance on a project. But it cannot be denied that your self-image has a very strong impact on your happiness, and your outlook on life can affect those around you. If you project a positive self-image, people will be more likely to see you as a positive, capable person.

I have seen that a top scorer self image about himself is very positive. He sees himself doing well every time whenever he appears for the test and hence is able to manifest positive results.

What does self image have to do with self esteem?

Self Esteem is how you feel about yourself. Image is about how you see yourself and how you believe others see you. They are closely connected because if you have a poor opinion of yourself your self esteem will be low.

You can't touch it, but it affects how you feel. You can't see it, but it's there when you look at yourself in the mirror. You can't hear it, but it's there every time you talk about yourself. What is this important but mysterious thing? It's yourself-esteem!

It's how you see yourself and how you feel about your achievements. Self-esteem isn't bragging about how great you are. It's more like quietly knowing that you're worth a lot (priceless, infact!). It's not about thinking you're perfect — because nobody is — but knowing that you're worthy of being loved and accepted.

Why Self-Esteem Is Important?

Self-esteem isn't like a cool pair of sneakers that you'd love to have but don't have to have. A student needs to have self-esteem.

Good self- esteem is important because it helps you to hold your head high and feel proud of yourself and what you can do. It gives you the courage to try new things and the power to believe in yourself. It lets you respect yourself, even when you make mistakes. And when you respect yourself, adults and other kids usually respect you, too.

Boosting Your Self-Esteem?

Of course it's Okay to have ups and downs in your feelings, but having low self-esteem isn't OK. Feeling like you're not important can make you sad and can keep you from trying new things. It can keep you from making friends or hurt how you do at school.

Having strong self-esteem is also a very big part of growing up. As you get older and face tough decisions— especially under peer pressure — the more self-esteem you have, the better. It's important to know you're worth a lot.

If you think you might have low self-esteem, try talking to an adult you trust about it. He or she may be able to help you come up with some good ideas for building your self-esteem.

In the meantime, here are a few things that you can try to increase your self-esteem:

• Make a list of the stuff you're good at. It can be anything from drawing or singing to playing a sport or telling a good joke. If you're having trouble with your list, ask your mom or dad to help you with it. Then add a few things to the list that you'd like to be good at. Your mom or dad can help you plan a way to work on those skills or talents.

• Give yourself three compliments everyday. Don't just say, "I'm so great." Be specific about something good about yourself, like, "I was a good friend today" or "I did better on that test than I thought I would." While you're at it, before you go to bed every night, list three things in your day that really made you happy.

• Remember that your body is your own, no matter what shape, size, or colour it is. If you are worried about your weight or size, you can check with your doctor to make sure that things are Okay. Remind yourself of things about your body that are cool, like, "My legs are strong and I can skate really well."

• Remember that there are things about yourself you can't change. You should accept and love these things such as skin colour and shoe size — because they are part of you.

• When you hear negative comments in your head, tell yourself to stop. When you do this, you take the power away from the voice inside that discourages you.

By focusing on the good things you do and all your great qualities, you learn to love and accept yourself — the main ingredients for strong self-esteem! Even if you've got room for improvement (and who doesn't?), realizing that you're valuable and important helps your self-esteem to shine.

Low self-esteem could lead to extremes of behaviour. A person with high self-esteem could choose identical behaviour for different reasons: He may be alone because he prefers solitude, whereas a person with low self-esteem prefers to be alone because he is uncomfortable in groups.

Some characteristics of people with:

High Self Esteem	Low Self Esteem
Talk about ideas	Talk about people
Caring attitude	Critical attitude
Humility	Arrogance
Respects authority	Rebels against authority
Courage of conviction	Goes along to get along
Confidence	Confusion
Concerned about character	Concerned about reputation
Assertive	Aggressive
Accepts responsibility	Blames the whole world
Self-interest	Selfish
Optimistic	Fatalistic
Understanding	Greedy
Willing to learn	Know it all
Sensitive	Touchy
Solitude	Lonely
Discuss	Argue
Believes in self-worth	Believes in net worth only
Guided	Misguided
Discipline	Distorted sense of freedom
Internally driven	Externally driven
Respects others	Looks down on others
Enjoys decency	Enjoys vulgarity
Knows limit	Evert thing goes
Giver	Taker

The objective of this list is to provide a basis for self evaluation rather than produce guilt. It is not necessary to have all the traits. Some characteristics may be present to a greater or lesser degree. So as long as we are able to recognize them we can make efforts to correct ourselves

Twelve Steps to Raise Your Self Esteem

Step One

Stop comparing yourself with other people. There will always be some people who have more than you and some who have less. If you play the comparison game, you'll run into too many "opponents" you can't defeat.

Step Two

Stop putting yourself down. You can't develop high self-esteem if you repeat negative phrases about yourself and your abilities. Whether speaking about your appearances, your career, your relationships, your financial situation, or any other aspects of your life, avoid self-deprecating comments.

Step Three

Accept all compliments with "thank you." Ever received a compliment and replied," Oh, it was nothing."When you reject a compliment, the message you give yourself is that you are not worthy of praise. Respond to all compliments with a simple Thank You."

Step Four

Use affirmations to enhance your self-esteem. On the back of a business card or small index card, write out a statement such as "I like and accept myself." or "I am valuable, lovable person and deserve the best in life." Carry the card with you. Repeat the statement several times during the day, especially at night before going to bed and after getting up in the morning. Whenever you say the affirmation, allow yourself to experience positive feelings about your statement.

Step Five

Take advantage of workshops, books on self- esteem. Whatever material you allow to dominate mind will eventually take root and affect your behaviour. If you watch negative television programs or read newspaper reports of murders and business rip off; you will grow cynical and pessimistic. Similarly, if you read books or listen to programs, that are positive in nature, you will take on these characteristics.

Step Six

Associate with positive, supportive people. When you are surrounded by negative people who constantly put you and your ideas down, your self- esteem is lowered. On the other hand, when you are accepted and encouraged, you feel better about yourself in the best possible environment to raise your self-esteem.

Step Seven

Make a list of your past successes. This doesn't necessarily have to consist of monumental accomplishments. It can include your "minor victories," like learning to skate, graduating from high school, receiving an award or promotion, reaching a business goal, etc. Read this list often. While reviewing it, close your eyes and recreate the feelings of satisfaction and joy you experienced when you first attained each success.

Step Eight

Make a list of your positive qualities. Are you honest? Unselfish? Helpful? Creative? Be generous with yourself and write down atleast 20 positive qualities. Again, it's important to review this list often. Most people dwell on their inadequacies and then wonder why their life isn't working out. Start focusing on your positive traits and you'll stand a much better chance of achieving what you wish to achieve.

Step Nine

Start giving more. I'm not talking about money. Rather, I mean that you must begin to give more of yourself to those around you. When you do things for others, you are making a positive contribution and you begin to feel more valuable, which, in turn, lifts your spirits and raises your own self-esteem.

StepTen

Get involved in work and activities you love. It's hard to feel good about yourself if your days are spent in work you despise. Self-esteem flourishes when you are engaged in work and activities that you enjoy and make you feel valuable. Even if you can't explore alternative career options at the present time, you can still devote leisure time to hobbies and activities, which you find stimulating and enjoyable.

Step Eleven

Be true to yourself. Live your own life- not the life others have decided is best for you. You'll never gain your own respect and feel good about yourself if you aren't leading the life you want to lead. If you're making decisions based on getting approval from friends and relatives, you aren't being true to yourself and your self-esteem is lowered.

Step Twelve

Take action! You won't develop high self-esteem if you sit on the sidelines and back away from challenges. When you take action - regardless of the ensuing result - you feel better about yourself. When you fail to move forward because of fear and anxiety, you'll be frustrated and unhappy - and you will undoubtedly deal a damaging blow to your self-esteem.

Creative Visualization

And

Imagination

"Limitations are within our minds, and it is upto us to rise above them."

Creative Visualization and Imagination

From Imagination to Reality-Attracting Success with Mind Power

According to Wikipedia Creative Visualization is a powerful mental technique to affect the outer world by changing one's thought. Creative Visualization is the basic technique underlying positive thinking and is frequently used by athletes to enhance their performance.

Creative visualization is the technique of using one's imagination to visualize specific behaviours or events occurring in one's life. Advocates suggest creating a detailed schema of what one desires and then visualizing it over and over again with all of the senses (i.e., what do you see? what do you feel? What do you hear? what does it smell like?). For example, in sports a golfer may visualize the "perfect" stroke over and over again to mentally train muscle memory. In one of the most well-known studies on Creative Visualization in sports, Russian scientists compared four groups of Olympic athletes in terms of their training schedules:

- *Group 1 - 100%physicaltraining;*
- *Group 2 - 75%physical training with 25% mental training;*
- *Group 3 - 50%physical training with 50% mental training;*
- *Group 4 - 25%physical training with 75% mental training.*

Group 4, with 75% of their time devoted to mental training, performed the best."The Soviets had discovered that mental images can act as a prelude to muscular impulses."

By visualizing a certain event or a situation, or an object, such as a car, a house, furniture etc, we attract it into our life. For some people it might look like magic, but there is no magic involved, only the natural process of the power of thoughts and natural mental laws. It is like having a genie at your disposal!

There are people who use this technique naturally in their everyday affairs, not being aware that they are using some sort of power. All successful people use it consciously or unconsciously, attracting the success they want into their life, by visualizing their goals as already accomplished.

All top scorer visualize there results in advance and the visualization is so powerful that they can actually see the exact percentage as well.
Creative Visualization and the Power of Thoughts
How does it work and why? Thoughts, if powerful enough, are accepted by our subconscious mind, which then changes our mindset accordingly, as well as our habits and actions, and this brings us into contact with new people, situations and circumstances.
Thought is a creative stuff that moulds our life and attracts similar stuff into our life. Thoughts also travel from one mind to another, and if they are strong enough, they can be unconsciously picked up by people, who are in a position to help us materialize our desires and goals.

Thought is energy, especially a concentrated thought laden with emotional energy. Thoughts change the balance of energy around us, and bring changes to the environment in accordance with them.
According to the Indian philosophy" Advaita- Vedanta", which is called "Non duality" in the West, the world is not real, but only an illusion, created by our thoughts. Since most people think and repeat the same or similar thoughts often, focusing their mind and thoughts on their current environment, they create and recreate the same sort of events or circumstances. This process preserves the same "world" and status quo.
It is like watching the same film over and over again, but we can change the film by changing our thoughts and visualize different circumstances and life, and in this way create a different "reality". For us it is a reality, though in fact it is just a dream we call "reality".
By changing our thoughts and mental images we change our "Reality"; we change the "illusory" world we believe we live in. We are not employing magic or supernatural powers when creating and changing

our life and circumstances. It is not something "Material" that we change; we only change our thoughts, which shape our world.

All this is like dreaming a very realistic dream, and then changing the dream. We are not awakening from the dream, just changing the dream. So why not change your dreams to something more satisfying?

If you live in small apartment and need a larger one, instead of brooding about your fate and lack of money, change your thoughts and visualize and believe that you are living in a bigger apartment.

Overcoming Limited Thinking

Creative visualization can do great things, but for every person there are some areas, which he or she might find hard to change, atleast in the immediate future. The power of visualization is a mighty power, but there are some limits to using it. These limits are within us, not in the power.

We often limit ourselves and cannot look beyond a limited circle. We limit ourselves by our thoughts and beliefs. The more open-minded we can be, and the more big we dare to think, the greater are our opportunities and possibilities. Limitations are within our minds, and it is upto us to rise above them.

It may take some time until things start to change. Simple, small demonstrations of this power may come fast, but bigger results may need a longer time to happen.

The time and effort put for thin this study are really worthwhile. Have faith and patience and results will start appearing.

How Do I Do It?

The First Step is to relax. Sit or lie in a comfortable position, and make a conscious effort to feel each part of your body relaxing. As you do this, takes low, deep breaths. This should take a few minutes. Another term for this is meditation. If you would like to learn more about it, you can find many self-help books and tapes which teach you how to do it!

The second step is to visualize. Many people can't "see" a mental picture at first, so if this happens don't let it worry you. After you've relaxed, you can "practice "visualizing by picturing things you see and do in everyday life. Try to imagine enjoyable things. You might picture your favourite room, or dancing with someone special, or eating your favourite meal. Doing these practice runs will help you "see" when it comes time to try the real thing!

These are the two basic steps, but now let's break it down a bit. You may want to work on these for awhile before trying your first real Visualization.

When you are ready to give it a try, you will need to do these very important things.

Decide what it is that you want. Is there something you want to change about yourself? Do you want a better career ?Do you want better health? You pick your goal. You will probably want to start with "easier" goals. Ones that you believe can happen in a timely manner. You can then work upto "harder" ones.

Next, picture the idea or object exactly as you want it to be. Picture yourself in the situation or using the object as if you already possessed it. Make sure you see this very clearly. You might also draw the scene to reinforce the idea, although, this step is not necessary.

Once you've got the picture in your head, think of it often. Not only when you are relaxing or meditating, but throughout the day as well. This is the process of sending that positive energy out into the universe. Remember the old saying "You reap what you sow"? Well, you're "sowing" when you think of what you want. The more positive energy you send out, the more you will get back.

Lastly, BELIEVE that the object is yours or will be yours. Any disbelief is negative energy and will counteract what you're trying to achieve.

And once you see it come true, acknowledge that you made it happen! Give yourself a pat on the back!

You now have the basic information to transform your life!

<u>**Success strategies to be a top scorer**</u>

<u>Success strategies to be a top scorer</u>

I)   Motivation &concentration

"I've been studying for 2 hours, but can't even remember what I read
five minutes ago!"
Many students struggle with making their study time more productive.
Here are some ways to improve efficiency.

First things first...Identify your distracters!
In order to get the most out of your study time, you have to pay close
attention to what you are doing. Distracters are those things or thoughts
which draw your attention away from your immediate task.
When you sit down to study, what distracts you? Take a moment to
identify 5 distracters that affected your most recent study time. Write
them down now.

1.   _____
2.   _____
3.   _____
4.   _____
5.   _____

Having identified your distracters, you are now in the position to deal
with them. Looking back at your list, try to categorise your distracters
into 'THINGS' or 'THOUGHTS'.

To deal with distracting THINGS, you can do the following:
a)   Define your own study area and keep it clear.
b)   Keep yourself away from potential attention-stealers.
c)   Put your phone on silent mode (don't even think of whatsapp),
and stay away from the computer if you get tend to get distracted with
thoughts of surfing the Internet, playing computer games,

d)   Many students are curious about the effect of music on studying
Is it a distraction, or an aid? Well research shows soothing music like
nature sound music e.g. sea waves, birds etc increases concentration. Do
not hear music with heart– pounding beats or music which contains
lyrics while studying as they distract your attention.

II)   Make a list of 'THINGS TO DO LATER'.

III)   Time-management or self-management?

Ever heard the saying, "Manage your time, or it will manage you"? This
is true. On the other hand, you can't really manage time, because it is at
no one's command – everyone has 24 hours a day, 168 hours a week.
So, you can only manage yourself around the time.

With regards to exam preparation, here are some important
considerations:

IV)   Plan in small blocks

E.g., plan hourly blocks. You will only be able to really concentrate for a
maximum of 45minutes, so plan a 15-minute break after that. (But
remember: 45/15, not 15/45!)

V)   Plan with precision
- Indicate exactly what you plan to achieve within that time.
- Example of planning with precision

-"Maths" 2 - 4pm;
- "Science" 5 - 7pm.
-"Maths – Chapter 4: Quadratic Equation – Word Problems";
- "Biology –Chapter 10: prokaryotic transcription"

VI)   Plan with the end in mind
•   Start from your goal. Check your exam timetable and work
backward from there. In the run-upto the exam, set specific targets to
complete by each week.
•   Need a weekly planner?
•   Break your study into bite-sized tasks which are more
manageable; in this way you would have accomplished something
tangible by the end of the time-limit.
- E.g. Science: Electrolysis of fused alumina

VII)   Plan with your strengths in mind
•   When are you the most productive, or at your mental best –
morning, afternoon, or night? Use these times to study your more
difficult subjects. Use your down-times to do more mechanical tasks,
such as laundry, cooking, or grocery shopping (but don't get carried
away!).

You probably would not need to divide your time equally between all
your subjects. In deciding how much time you want to allocate for each
subject, consider the following:
•   Amount of study you have done during the semester;
•   How difficult you perceive the subject to be;
•   Weightage of the exam;
•   How well you hope to do in it. Get started with a blank daily
planner!

VIII)   Plan with flexibility
•   This might seem contradictory to the point above, but what it
means is that you shouldn't plan a time-table that's so packed, that it
leaves you with no buffer time to perform everyday activities (you still

need to eat, rest, travel, and take showers!) and to deal with unforeseen emergencies.

• Think of your schedule as the means to an end, not an end in itself. Some students prefer to operate on a more 'elastic' time-schedule, as they feel unable to commit themselves to hourly blocks. If this describes you, then what you can do is to set yourself specific, attain able task-goals for the day, and monitor your progress along the way. Write down your task-goals the night before, and keep them in front of you all the time. Check that you are on target.

IX) Reward yourself!

After you have accomplished each of the tasks you have set out to do, give yourself a break – go for a walk, watch some television, or catch up with your friend.

X) Know your content

XI) Start early to organize your readings, notes, and assignments.

XII) Pay attention to what is emphasized in lectures and tutorials.

This means attending lessons right upto the end! By listening carefully, you will be able to select and identify which topics you should spend more time on. Your lecturers will also tell you their expectations; since they are the ones who are going to mark your work, you'd better be listening!

XIII)   Take note of the formats of the different exams.

For all cases of exam format, unless your lecturer says otherwise, it is advantageous to practice with past year papers. This is not so much so that you can spot questions', but more importantly, so that you will be familiarized with the paper, and can practice answering different questions. You do not win a lottery for finishing first. Use all the time that is given to you.

Lakshya–developing your goals

What you get by achieving your goals is not as important as what you
become by achieving your goals.

-ZigZiglar

Before we start of with this chapter list your 3 goals in order of priority.

Goal# 1: _____

List atleast 5 reasons why you want to achieve this goal.

_____

_____

List atleast 5 activities which you do daily to achieve this goal.

_____

_____

Goal # 2: _____

List atleast 5 reasons why you want to achieve this goal.

_____

_____

List at least 5 activities which you do daily to achieve this goal.

_____

_____

Goal # 3 _____

List atleast 5 reasons why you want to achieve this goal.

_____

_____

List atleast 5 activities which you do daily to achieve this
Goal._____ _____

_____

Imagine that you are a football player and you are the captain of your team. Visualize yourself in a match with another team. The match has been started. What will be the next thing in your mind? You might say, 'Obviously to make a goal and win the match'. It's the constant thought in your mind even though you are passing or dodging the ball while running towards the goal.

It's the similar thing with our life. The ball is nothing but our career, our life. Many of you are there on the ground competing with the competitive world with the missing goal-net. Imagine what will happen to the football match if the goal-net is not there? What will be the result of such match? Many of you are just standing on the ground with the ball wondering what to do with it! What will happen to match if you start playing without practicing it? What will happen to the match if you don't learn the strategies and skill required to play? The answer is pretty simple you lose the match i.e. you don't succeed in your life and then you wonder why it is happening with you! Is it a coincident that other person won? No its not, this person is better prepared, has Goal setting skills and strategies, time management skills but I always wonder why people say that it was his luck...

Goal setting is a powerful process for thinking about your ideal future, and for motivating yourself to turn this vision of the future into reality. The process of setting goals helps you choose where you want to go in life. By knowing precisely what you want to achieve, you know where you have to concentrate your efforts. You'll also quickly spot the distractions that would otherwise lure you from your course.

More than this, properly-set goals can be incredibly motivating, and as you get into the habit of setting and achieving goals, you'll find that your self-confidence builds fast.

Once you have set your goals, and then create a daily to-do list of things that you should do today to work towards your lifetime goals. At an early stage these goals may be to read books and gather information on the achievement of your goals. This will help you to improve the quality and realism of your goal setting.

Your Goals must be SMART

A useful way of making goals more powerful is to use the SMART mnemonic. SMART usually stands for:

S - Specific. In addition to specific, don't stretching, systematic, synergistic, significant and shifting round out the picture?

M- Measurable but I also recommend meaningful, memorable, motivating and even, magical.

A – Attainable but A also needs to stand for action plans, accountability, acumen and agreed-upon.

R- Relevant but it also stands for realistic, reasonable, resonating, results-oriented, rewarding, responsible, reliable, rooted in facts and remarkable.

T- Time-bound and it also represents timely, tangible and thoughtful. For example, instead of having "to sail around the world" as a goal, it is more powerful to say "To have completed my trip around the world by December 31, 2015." Obviously, this will only be attainable if a lot of preparation has been completed beforehand!

The following broad guidelines will help you to set effective goals:

• State each goal as a positive statement: Express your goals positively
- 'Execute this technique well' is a much better goal than 'Don't make this stupid mistake.'
• Be precise: Set a precise goal, putting in dates, times and amounts so that you can measure achievement. If you do this, you will know exactly when you have achieved the goal, and can take complete satisfaction from having achieved it.
• Set priorities: When you have several goals, give each a priority. This helps you to avoid feeling overwhelmed by too many goals, and helps to direct your attention to the most important ones

- Write goals down: This crystallizes them and gives them more force.
- Keep operational goals small: Keep the low-level goals you are working towards small and achievable. If a goal is too large, then it can seem that you are not making progress towards it. Keeping goals small and incremental gives more opportunities for reward. Derive today's goals from larger ones.
- If you learnt something that would lead you to change other goals, do so.
- If you noticed a deficit in your skills despite achieving the goal, decide whether to set goals to fix this.

Failure to meet goals does not matter much, as long as you learn from it. Feed lessons learned back into your goal setting program. Remember too that your goals will change as time goes on. Adjust them regularly to reflect grow thin your knowledge and experience, and if goals do not hold any attraction any longer, then let them go.

Reviewing your goals daily is a crucial part of your success and must become part of your routine. Each morning when you wake up read your list of goals that are written in the positive. Visualize the completed goal, see the new home, smell the leather seats in your new car, feel the cold hard cash in your hands. Then each night, right before you go to bed, repeat the process. This process will start both your subconscious and conscious mind on working towards the goal. This will also begin to replace any of the negative self-talk you may have and replace it with positive self-talk.

Every time you make a decision during the day, ask yourself this question, "Does it take me closer to, or further from my goal." If the answer is "closer to," then you've made the right decision. If the answer is "further from," well, you know what to do.

If you follow this process everyday you will be on your way to achieving unlimited success in every aspect of your life.

Rewrite your 3 goals in order of priority after reading the chapter.

Goal# 1:_____
List atleast 5 reasons why you want to achieve this goal.
_____
_____

List atleast 5 activities which you do daily to achieve this goal.
_____
_____

Goal # 2:_____
List atleast 5 reasons why you want to achieve this
goal._____
_____ _____

List atleast 5 activities which you do daily to achieve this
goal._____ _____
_____

Goal# 3:_____
List atleast 5 reasons why you want to achieve this
goal._____
_____ _____

List at least 5 activities which you do daily to achieve this
goal._____ _____
_____

Time Management

Time Management Skills

 Do you fall behind in your home work and other school activities? Are you one of the student who is not able to finish your studies even one minute before exam? If 24 hours in one day seem in sufficient to you to complete your work, don't think
That you are a dull student, you just need some preparation and training in time management. You can achieve your daily goals efficiently by practicing time management skills.
Mismanagement of time is a common problem found in schools students. When students do not find enough time for studies or they stress out due to lack of good results, it shows how poorly they manage their time.
Below are some suggestions on how best you can manage your time and start organizing your messy and hectic life.

Here are the calculations for a typical week:

Total available hours 24 hours X 7 days   =168hours Minus Average sleep 7 hours X 7days =49hours Total waking hours
          =119hours Average time at school 6 hoursX6days
          =36hours
AveragetimeatClasses3hoursX6days   = 18hours
Averagetimecommuting1 hoursX6days   = 6hours
Total school/classes time   =60hours

Free time available after accounting
for school/classes time
and sleep time   =(119-60)=59hours

Total work time as % of waking hours 50% approximately

Time availability, therefore, isn't an issue. Most important thing is "how to take control of your time and therefore, your life"

Before we start with time management make a list of things which you did yesterday.

5 a.m: _____
6 a.m: _____
7.am: _____
8.am: _____
9 am: _____
10am: _____
11am: _____
12pm: _____
1pm:_____
2pm: _____
3pm: _____
4pm: _____
5pm: _____
6pm: _____
7pm: _____
8pm: _____
9pm: _____
10pm:_____
11pm: _____

After having listed all the activities fill up the Time Matrix on the next page according to the importance and urgency in different quadrants. It applies to any field you want to succeed at.
Basics you have to start somewhere, and these tips can help you learn the basics of time management.

1. Write things down. With so much going on it's hard to remember every little thing you have to do — unless you write it down of course.

2. Don't take too many hours. Unless you're ultra ambitious, taking more than18 hours a semester is unnecessary and will result in extra stress and less time to concentrate on each class. Take a reasonable amount of classes each semester so you won't feel completely overwhelmed.

3. Stay organized. You'll save yourself loads of time later by staying organized from the get-go.

4. Focus on one thing at a time. Multitasking may seem like a good idea, but really you'll get more done by focusing your energy on one task at a time. Once you've finished one thing you can check it off your list and move on to the next.

5. Take charge of your time. At the end of the day, only one person has control over how you spend your time, and that's you. Take charge of your day, get important things done and learn to say no if you have to.

6. Resist the urge to procrastinate. The world is full of distractions, and to really be effective at managing your time you have to find a way to ignore them when it counts. Give yourself little breaks as rewards for not putting of tasks.

7. Avoid taking classes on material you've already learned. This may seem like a "well duh" sort of thing, but don't take classes for the things you already know. Also don't take too many classes for same subject. Instead take a test on these subjects. This will save lot of time.

8. Get an early start to your day. Students aren't usually known as early bird types, but you can be doing yourself a huge favour by getting up early on weekly offs and when every you have holidays. You'll have more time during the day to work on home work and study, which will leave your evenings free to do things you enjoy.

9. Learn material the first time around. If you don't understand something in your classes don't just gloss over it and assume you'll learn it later. Take the time to ensure you learn it the first time. It can help you to more easily understand concepts that follow and will save you the time of revisiting the topic later.

10.Control your surroundings. While you can't always make your study environment distraction free, you can do your best to create an environment that is most conducive to getting work done.

11.Have confidence in your abilities. Sometimes your schedule will seem almost impossible. Have confidence that you can do things, and you may surprise yourself when you truly step up to the challenge. You'll never know how much you can do unless you test yourself, so give yourself opportunities to shine, even under pressure.

12. Get the most out of class. If you're just going to class to sleep or talk to you friends, you're wasting time you could be using to do other things.
Read over class materials ahead of time so you have a rough idea of what class will be about. This will allow you to concentrate on the elements of the lessons that are truly important and make it easier for you to study in the future.

13. Know what's important to you. Everyone has a different idea of what they want to take out of school/college. Some people want to get perfect grades and others are more concerned with making friends and building relationships. Figure out what things are most important to you and concentrate the bulk of your energies on those studying While you may not have that many hours of classes each week, you still have to account for the time you'll need to spend studying for them. Here are some tips on how you can fit your study time into your schedule.

14. Take advantage of downtime. If you take along bus ride each day or have some spare time why not use it to get a little studying in? The less time you waste during downtime, the more time you'll have later.

15. Set goals. It can be hard to get motivated to study when you don't have a clear goal in mind. Set a goal of how much you want to get done and try your best to meet it.

16. Use the syllabus. Your syllabus will let you know when and how fast you'll be covering topics in your class. You can use it to get ahead when you have extra time or to know when and what you'll need to work on each day to keep up.

17.Work to boost your memory. You'll spend much less time studying if you can remember what you study the first time around. Easier said than done, however, but you can play games, read books and eat foods that will help keep you at your maximum memory potential.

18. Learn what works for you. Different methods work better for different people. If you're struggling with a certain way you've been studying, try something else. You may find it takes you less time and that you get a lot more out o fit by making a simple change.

19. Study difficult subjects first. There's no sense in putting off the worst for last—it will only encourage you to procrastinate and get less done in the long run. Get the hard stuff out of the way and you'll have a much happier rest of the day.

20. Work in short blocks with breaks. You won't be doing yourself any favours by pulling marathon study sessions with no breaks. Studies have shown that the most effective way to get through material is to go through it in smaller sessions and to give your mind and eyes time to rest in between with short breaks.

21.Team up with classmates. There's no need to study alone if you can get more out of working with your classmates. Sometimes collaboration Can be a much faster way to get through material, and it can be a great help if you're struggling with certain concepts. Just make sure your study sessions don't get too off track.

22. Avoid skipping class. While everyone skips a class now and then to catch upon sleep or to get other things done they feel are more pressing, try not to make a habit of it. Going to class will make it easier for you to keep up with the material and will give you the chance to ask questions.

23. Create a strategy. You'll get the most out of your study time if you go into it with a strategy in mind. Focus on certain subjects first or spend a little extra time on topics that you struggle with. Whatever you do, make sure it works for you and makes the most of your time. Homework: Homework is rarely fun but you still need to get it done, and the sooner the better. Here are some tips on making homework as painless and time- friendly as possible.

24. Prioritize.
If you've got a number of homework assignments, focus on the ones that are due the soonest or that will take you the most time first. Once you get those out of the way you'll feel better about concentrating on the others.

25.Don't wait until the last minute. While for most people this is easier said than done, waiting until the last minute to complete homework is not only stressful but it can mean that you get a lot less out of the work that you put in. Give yourself enough leeway with time to ensure you won't have to rush around to get things done.

26 .Get ahead if you can. If you find that you have some extra time in your day, use it to get ahead in the classes that you can. You'll thank

yourself later, on a day when you have loads of extra work to do and you'll have one less thing to worry about.

27. Assign a specific amount of time the project should take. One way to keep yourself moving forward and not to waste time is to assign a specific amount of time that you think a project should take and try to fit it into that timeframe. Sometimes this isn't always possible, but if you know about how long it takes you to complete a certain kind of assignment, it can help keep you on task.

28. Find your peak hours. Everyone has hours of the day when they simply perform better mentally. Figure out what your peak times are, and do your hardest work during these times so that you'll have the energy to get through them more quickly.

29. Break up large projects. Don't let yourself get overwhelmed with huge research projects. Break them up into sections which will be easier to tackle and will allow you to complete a small part of the project each day.

30. Work smarter. You don't have to work harder to get more done, just smarter. If you know you have two projects that need research at the library, work on both at the same time and save yourself an extra trip.

31. Set mini deadlines. If you know you're a chronic procrastinator, you can help keep yourself working on home work assignments, especially larger ones, by creating mini-deadlines within the assignment. This will help to keep you working through the assignment and prevent it from all having to be done at the last minute.

32. Ask for help. Sometimes you'll have assignments that you simply won't understand no matter how many times you look through them. While figuring things out on your own is rewarding, at a certain point it

can be much more time efficient to simply ask for help from your professors or classmates.

33.Don't put off projects you're dreading. No one wants to think about starting again to research projects that isn't due until the end of these muster. The problem is that projects like these usually get put off until the end of the semester, and then you have very little time to put them together. If you're dreading a project, do it little by little or just get it out of the way all at once. You'll feel a million times better once it's out of the way and you won't have to worry about it anymore.

Scheduling, It's essential for time management that you keep a schedule and stick to it.

<u>Power of Concentration</u>

I never could have done what I have done without the habits of punctuality, order, and diligence, without the determination to concentrate myself on one subject at a time...

-Charles Dickens

Power of Concentration

A well known story about Arjuna exemplifies his power of concentration. Guru Dronacharya once decided to test his students in their skill of archery. He hung a wooden bird from the branch of a tree and then summoned his students. He asked the first one to aim for the bird's eye but not shoot just yet. He then asked the student what the student could see. The student replied that he could see the garden, the tree, flowers, etc. Drona asked him to step aside and not shoot. He repeated the same process with a few other students. When it was Arjuna's turn, Arjuna told his Guru that the only thing he could see was the bird's eye. This satisfied the Guru and he allowed Arjuna to shoot the bird. The lesson here is the power of focus. Arjuna once noticed his brother, Bhima, who was a voracious eater, eating in the dark as though it was daylight, and realized that if he could practice archery in the dark he would be a master.

When I was a child, I saw how a magnifying glass could burn a piece of paper, when the rays of the sun were focused through it. The fire could start only when the sun's rays were concentrated to a small point. When the magnifying glass was moved too far away or too close to the paper, the rays were not focused enough and nothing happened. This experience describes vividly the power of concentration.

This power can be described as focused attention. It is the ability to direct the attention to one single thought or subject, to the exclusion of everything else.

When our mind is focused, our energies are not dissipated on irrelevant activities or thoughts. This is why developing concentration is essential to anyone who aspires to take charge of his or her life. This skill is essential for every kind of success. Without it, our efforts gets scattered, but with it, we can accomplish great things.

Do you now realize why it is very important and worthwhile to develop and improve the ability to concentrate?

To develop this power you need to train and exercise it. Forget all your excuses about not having the time or being too busy. Do not say that the circumstances are not appropriate or that you cannot find a quiet place to exercise. With a little planning, desire and motivation you can always find the time to exercise each day, no matter how busy you are.

Look at the following familiar situation. You need to study something for your job or for an exam. You sit comfortably on the sofa with the book in your hands and start reading. After a while you feel hungry and go to the kitchen to eat something.

You return to read, and then hear some people talking outside. You listen to them for several moments and then bring your attention back to the book.

After a while you feel restless and switch on the radio to listen to some music. You continue to read for a little while, and then remember something that happened yesterday, and you start thinking about it. When you look at your watch, you are amazed to find out that one complete hour has passed and you have hardly read anything.

This is what happens when one lacks concentration. Imagine what you could have accomplished, if you could control your attention and focus your mind!

Work that requires physical strength, such as carrying heavy loads for example, develops physical strength. Yet, it is not as exercising daily to the gym in a systematic manner. It is the same with concentration. Reading, studying and trying to pay attention to what we do, develops some of this ability, but practicing exercises diligently each day is something else, it is like training in a gym.

Inner resistance to developing concentration

In order to develop this ability we have to train our minds. Most people think that concentration is a strenuous and tiring activity, and that it involves exertion and tension, which are difficult and unpleasant.

This belief starts at an early age. Parents and teachers expect children to study, do their homework and get good grades. This brings up feeling of being coerced and forced to do something a child doesn't like to do. When they are too often told that they are not concentrating well enough, they develop a loathing for concentration, and often for studying too. These become associated with coercion, lack of freedom, doing something they do not like to do, and which is against their will. When they grow up, it is no wonder that their powers of concentration are weak, and they have no desire to strain their minds.

Though most people acknowledge the fact that good concentration is a great asset, yet most of them do nothing to strengthen it, mostly because they don't know how. Reading and thinking about its benefits, and about the reasons why it should be cultivated, can help to change the attitude towards it.

Concentration can be fun if approached in the right way. It should be practiced with joy, fun, optimism, and understanding of its great possibilities. It has to be approached in a positive manner and then success dawns.

Concentration exercises

Exercise1
Take a book and count the words in any one paragraph. Count them again to be sure that you have counted them correctly. Start with one paragraph and when it becomes easier, count the words in a whole page. Perform the counting mentally and only with your eyes, without pointing your finger at each word.

Exercise2
Count backwards in your mind, from one hundred to one.

Exercise3

Count in your mind from one hundred to one, skipping each three numbers, that is
100,97,94,etc.

Exercise4

Choose an inspiring word, or just a simple sound, and repeat it silently in your mind for five minutes. When your mind can concentrate more easily, try to reach ten minutes of uninterrupted concentration.

Exercise5

Take a fruit, an apple for example, and look at it from all sides. Concentrate your attention on it and examine it from all sides. Devote the whole session to concentrating on it. Do not be carried away by irrelevant thoughts that arise. Stay with the apple. It could be any other fruit. Look at it and do not think about the shop were you bought it, about the way it is grown, its nutritive value etc, only about the object in front of you. Just look at it, see it, smell it and touch it.

Exercise6

This is the same as exercise number 5, only that this time you visualize the fruit with your eyes closed. Start by performing again exercise number 5 for five minutes, and then do this one. Try to see, feel, taste, smell the fruit in your imagination. Try to see a clear and well defined image. If difficulties arise open your eyes, look at the fruit, close them again and continue the exercise.

Exercise 7

Take a small simple object such as a spoon, a fork, or a glass. Concentrate on one of these objects. Watch the object from all sides without any verbalization, that is, with no words in your mind. Just watch the object without thinking with words about it.

Exercise8

After becoming proficient in the above exercises, you can come to this exercise. Draw a small geometrical figure, about three inches in size, such as a triangle, a rectangle or a circle, paint it with any colour you wish, and concentrate on it. You should see only the figure, nothing else. Only the figure exists for you now, with no unrelated thoughts or any distractions. Try not to think with words during the exercise. Watch the figure in front of you and that's it. Try not to strain your eyes.

Exercise9

The same as number 8, only this time visualize the figure with the eyes closed. As before, if you forget how the figure looks like, open your eyes for a few seconds and watch the figure and then close your eyes and continue with the exercise.

Exercise10

The same as above in number 9 but the eyes open.

Exercise 11

Try for at least five minutes, to stay without thoughts. This exercise is to be attempted only after all the previous ones have been performed successfully. The previous exercises, if practiced correctly, will endow you with the ability to impose silence on your thoughts. In time it will become easier and easier.

The secret of success is constant practice. The more time you devote to the exercises the faster your success arrives. Go on gradually; ten minutes at the start and in time as you gain the ability to concentrate, give it more time. When you see that you are successful, you will begin to love the exercises, and in time they will become a habit. You will be able to concentrate your attention easily and effortlessly upon anything you want to concentrate on.

Stress Management for Students

Stress: Everybody knows what it is; no one knows what it is.

Stress Management for Students

Students are under enormous pressure, and they experience a great deal of stress. Keeping up with studies and making good grades is difficult in itself, but there are also the added parental and tuition/classes pressures .Our education system is as such that a student spent almost 12 hrs in school and tuition daily. It does not create an educated person rather a frustrated and stressed individual. On an average a student giving board exam spends 15 hrs per day only in studying. A student has to keep up with the homework of school along with the classes homework. Time is always running ahead. Subconsciously every student is in a war with Time and when everything becomes overwhelming stress takes its toll. Let's understand more about stress before managing it.

Cortisol is an important stress hormone in the body, secreted by the adrenal glands and involved in the following functions and more:

- Proper glucose metabolism
- Regulation of blood pressure
- Insulin release for blood sugar maintenance
- Immune function
- Inflammatory response

Normally, it's present in the body at higher levels in the morning, and at its lowest at night. Although stress isn't the only reason that cortisol is secreted into the blood stream, it has been termed "the stress hormone" because it's also secreted in higher levels during the body's 'fight or flight' response to stress i.e 'either fight or runaway from a danger', and is responsible for several stress-related changes in the body.

Higher and more prolonged levels of cortisol in the blood stream have been shown to have negative effects, such as:

- Impaired mental performance
- Suppressed thyroid function

- Blood sugar imbalances such as hyper-glycemia
- Decreased bone density
- Decrease in muscle tissue
- Higher blood pressure
- Lowered immunity and inflammatory responses in the body, slowed wound healing, and other health consequences
- Increased abdominal fat, which is associated with a greater amount of health problems than fat deposited in other areas of the body. Some of the health problems associated with increased stomach fat are heart attacks, strokes, the development of higher levels of "bad" cholesterol(LDL) and lower levels of "good" cholesterol(HDL), which can lead to other health problems!

Stress has become a part of life and the use of stress management techniques can make life easier and will keep cortisol levels healthy and under control.

There's nothing like a good story to help us get the point, so let me give you the Glass of Water theory of stress management here:

A lecturer, when explaining stress management to an audience, raise the glass of water and asked, "How heavy is this glass of water?"

Answers called out ranged from 250g to 500g.

The lecturer replied, "The absolute weight doesn't matter. It depends on how long you try to hold it. If I hold it for a minute, that's not a problem. If I hold it for an hour, I'll have an ache in my right arm. If I hold it for a day, you'll have to call an ambulance.

"In each case, it's the same weight, but the longer I hold it, the heavier it becomes." He continued, "And that's the way it is with stress management. If we carry our burdens all the time, sooner or later, as the burden becomes increasingly heavy, we won't be able to carry on.

"As with the glass of water, you have to put it down for a while and rest before holding it again. When we're refreshed, we can carry on with the burden.

"So, before you return home tonight, put the burden of work down. Don't carry it home. You can pick it up tomorrow. Whatever burdens you're carrying now, let them down for a moment if you can. "Relax; pick them up later after you've rested. Life is short. Enjoy it!"

Stress Management Tips

Not all stress management techniques are suitable for students because of the time involved. The following stress management techniques are not only some of the most common, but also are well suited to students:

Do not wait.

If you know that you have an assignment due or an exam looming on the horizon, do not wait until the last minute to open your text. By starting early and focusing on small amounts each day, you will be prepared for the exam or have the assignment finished well before the due date. When you wait until the last minute, you increase your stress and anxiety, and your performance typically suffers.

2. Perform routine maintenance.

Just as a car needs maintenance, like an oil change, your body needs its own version of routine maintenance. You need to eat regular, healthy meals and get plenty of rest. In addition, take personal time to take a walk, go out with friends, or do other activities that you enjoy. Taking care of you creates a more positive mood and better performance.

3. Exercise.

Physical exercise is not only good for your body, but it also serves to relieve stress. Engaging in physical activities increases your circulation, clears your mind, and boosts your overall energy level. Exercise also decreases levels of stress hormones, like cortisol, helping you to feel more relaxed. Of course, there is also the benefit of having a physical release for negative emotions, like anger or hostility.

4.Get organized.

One of the major factors in stress for students is lack of organization. Make a schedule that shows where you have to be and when, as well as when assignments are due and when exams are scheduled. Organize your study area so you can find books, notebooks, and pencils or pens quickly and easily. Simple organization will take care of missed deadlines and forgotten assignments, and it will prevent you from being stuck with starting assignments at the.

5.PowerNaps

Students, with their packed schedules, are notorious for missing sleep. Unfortunately, operating in a sleep-deprived state puts you at a distinct disadvantage. You're less productive, you may find it more difficult to learn, and you may even be a hazard behind the wheel! Learn more about the effects of sleep deprivation and the value of the powernap; for busy students, it's a must!

6.Breathing Exercise

When your body is experiencing a stress response, you're often not thinking as clearly as you could be. A quick way to calm down is to practice breathing exercises. These can be done virtually anywhere to relieve stress in minutes, and are especially effective for reducing anxiety before or even during tests, as well as during other times when stress feels overwhelming. Learn more about how to practice breathing exercises.

Breathing exercises are an ideal way to relieve stress in that they're fast, simple, free, and can be performed by just about anyone. They can also be done anywhere and at virtually anytime. These factors make stress relief breathing exercises one of my most popular and convenient tension tamers. Here's how basic controlled breathing works:

Time Required: You decide!

7.Music

A convenient stress reliever that has also shown many cognitive benefits, music can help you to relieve stress and either calm yourself down or stimulate your mind as your situation warrants. Students can harness the benefits of music by playing classical music while studying, playing upbeat music to 'wakeup' mentally, or relaxing with the help of their favourites low melodies.

8.EatRight

You may not realize it, but your diet can either boost your brain power or sap you of mental energy! While a healthy diet isn't generally thought of as a stress management technique or a study aid, it can actually function as both! Read more on the consequences of a poor diet, and learn how to relieve stress with a healthy diet. It takes virtually no extra time, and can keep you from experiencing diet-related mood swings, light-headedness and more.

Consequences of poor diet

Stress and Nutrition: Stress can be a problem in itself, of course. But stress can sometimes lead to unhealthy lifestyle patterns — which lead to more stress! For example, when we're harried and under stress, we tend to make poor food choices. Unfortunately, these food choices can create more stress in the long run, as well as other problems. As you read the following ways in which stress can affect our nutritional choices, ask yourself this: when feeling overwhelmed, have you found yourself doing any of the following?

• 　　　Drinking Too Much Coffee: When burning the candle at both ends, people often find themselves using coffee drinks to jump-start themselves in the morning, and a pattern of all-day coffee drinking often ensues.

• Eating The Wrong Foods: Due to partially increased levels of Cortisol, the stress hormone, stressed people tend to crave foods high in fat, sugar and salt. Think about it: how often have you turned to your good friends Ice cream and chocolates after a long, stressful day?

11.Positive Thinking and Affirmations
Did you know that optimists actually experience better circumstances, in part, because their way of thinking helps to create better circumstances in their lives?
It's true! The habit of optimism and positive thinking can bring better health, better relationships, and, yes, better grades. Learn how to train your brain for more positive self talk and a brighter future with affirmations and other tools for optimism.

How to read Textbooks effectively

How to read Text books effectively

SQRW is a four-step strategy for reading and taking notes from chapters in a textbook. Each letter stands for one step in the strategy. Using SQRW will help you to understand what you read and to prepare a written record of what you learned. The written record will be valuable when you have to participate in a class discussion and again when you study for a test. Read to learn what to do for each step in SQRW.

S - Survey.

Surveying brings to mind what you already know about the topic of a chapter and prepares you for learning more. To survey a chapter, read the title, introduction, headings, and the summary or conclusion. Also, examine all visuals such as pictures, tables, maps, and/or graphs and read the caption that goes with each. By surveying a chapter, you will quickly learn what the chapter is about.

Q - Question.

You need to have questions in your mind as you read. Questions give you a purpose for reading and help you stay focused on the reading assignment. Form questions by changing each chapter heading into a question. Use the words who, what, when, where, why, or how to form questions. For example, for the heading "Uses of Electricity" in a chapter about how science improves lives, you might form the question "What are some uses of electricity?" If a heading is stated as a question, use that question. When a heading contains more than one idea, form a question for each idea. Do not form questions for the Introduction, Summary, or Conclusion.

R - Read.

Read the information that follows each heading to find the answer to each question you formed. As you do this, you may decide you need to change a question or turn it into several questions to be answered. Stay focused and flexible so you can gather as much information as you need to answer each question.

W - Write.

Write each question and its answer in your notebook. Reread each of your written answers to be sure each answer is legible and contains all the important information needed to answer the question.

As you practice using SQRW, you will find you learn more and have good study notes to use to prepare for class participation and tests.

Strategy for Solving Math Word Problems

Strategy for Solving Math Word Problems

RQWQCQ is a good strategy to use when solving math word problems. Each of the letters in RQWQCQ stands for a step in the strategy.

R - Read
Read the entire problem to learn what it is about. You may find it helpful to read the problem out loud, form a picture of the problem in your mind, or draw a picture of the problem.

Q - Question
Find the question to be answered in the problem. Often the question is directly stated. When it is not stated, you will have to identify the question to be answered.

W - Write
Write the facts you need to answer the question. It is helpful to cross out any facts presented in the problem that are not needed to answer the question. Sometimes, all of facts presented in the problem are needed to answer the question.

Q - Question
Ask yourself "What computations must I do to answer the question?"

C - Compute
Setup the problem on paper and do the computations. Check your computations for accuracy and make any needed corrections. Once you have done this, circle your answer.

Q - Question

Look at your answer and ask yourself:"Is my answer possible?" You may find that your answer is not possible because it does not fit with the facts presented in the problem. When this happens, go back through the steps of RQWQCQ until you arrive at an answer that is possible.

M-U-R-D-E-R Study Technique

M-U-R-D-E-R Study Technique

I just bumped into a catchy acronym of a study technique called
M.U.R.D.E.R From Hayes, John R., The Complete Problem Solver book
which stands for Mood, Understand, Recall, Digest, Expand and Review.
And when I took a look unto it, the techniques are simple and very
doable making them handy for all students.

Mood–

This is the first thing you need to set when you are about to study. You
need to have a proper state of mind or disposition so that you can study
efficiently.

Understand–

Understand what you need to study and what are the things or topics
that you don't understand so that you can put more attention to that
particular subject.

Recall-

Check if you can recall what you have studied. Go back again to the
topics that you did not clearly get.

Digest–

After reading or studying each topic, digest what you have just read or
studied using your own words.

Expand –

Expand what you have studied by asking questions like "what questions
would I ask to the author or what criticism would I offer to him about
this topic? How could I apply this material to what I am interested in?
How could I make this information interesting and understandable to
other students?"

Review–

Review by going again to the readings you have to ensure that you have covered all the necessary topics you need to study.

Do's and Don'ts tips for academic success

Do's and Don'ts tips for academic success

If you desire greater academic success, there is no substitute for test preparation. Learning how to best prepare and study for exams will make you feel more relaxed heading into an exam, and the combination of preparation and relaxation will help you achieve greater success. So these are some of the key tips for test preparation and test-taking.

Do's	Don'ts
Do your best to plan far ahead of the test date so that you can block out plenty of study time	Don't cram the night before because the brain does not perform at its best if not given adequate rest resulting in stress and ultimately causes you to go blank during exam.
Do consider attending classes and completing your reading assignments well ahead of the test as part of your test-taking preparation. Both attending lectures and completing the reading assignments are essential aspects of test preparation and academic success	Don't let outside work whether a part- time job or extracurricular activities, sports affect your studying plans. And if they interfere, do find away to make up the studying.
Do use mnemonic devices, mind maps, or other tools for subjects that require remembering large quantities of information and inter-relationships	Don't waste too much time preparing to study for the exam; instead, spend the bulk of your time studying for the exam.

Do get information about all aspects of the test as you can—including the types of questions(true/false, multiple choice, short answer, and essay are the most common),the chapters/readings the test will cover, the amount of time you'll have to take the test, and any supporting materials you need to bring with you to the test.	Don't skip any test review sessions the professor schedules. Review sessions are great opportunities to ask questions, listen to the issues the professors thinks most relevant, and possibly gets molecules as to what to expect on the test.
Do set challenging, but realistic goals for each test. Having a goal will give you the motivation to help you with studying.	Don't get a goal that is beyond your reach and sets you up for disappointment.
Do take scheduled (and perhaps a few unscheduled) breaks while studying. Most college students say that studying in smaller chunks with regular breaks helps them retain more information and thus perform better on exams	Don't study in a place with lots of distractions, but do find the place that best works for you(such as your bedroom or apartment, the library, an empty classroom, etc.).Don't let outside influences affect your test- taking preparations .Whenever possible, keep roommate, family, and significant others relationships free of drama so that you can fully concentrate on preparing and taking the test.
Do review previous tests so that you have a better idea of the types of questions your professor ask (and how's/he asks them). Some professors place old test son reserve in the library. Finally, some student groups keep files of old tests.	Don't just review old exams, but do take atleast one practice exam. If your professor does not release old exams, check to see if the publisher of your textbook offers practice exams. Finally, if you at least know the types of questions to expect on the exam, You can develop your own practice exam.

Do pack up everything you need for the exam the night before so that you don't get in a panic for forgetting something(such as pencils, hall tickets, etc.).	Don't stay up late the night before an exam. Getting a good night's sleep will greatly enhance your test-taking abilities. And do watch your diet; eating well help your brain functions better.
Do arrive to class a few minutes early so that you can get situated comfortably in your seat and mentally prepare for the exam, but don't get caught up in any last-minute jitters from other students.	Don't ignore any directions you receive with the exam. Make certain You understand the test's instructions before you start taking it.
Do review the entire test and consider quickly performing a mind/brain dump --in which you write down relevant formulas, dates, processes, models etc., that you are afraid of forgetting as you work your way through the exam.	Don't allow yourself to get stuck on a question for too long; you must pace yourself so that you can complete the exam in time. When you are stumped by a question, try rewriting it. If that trick does not work, try asking your professor to rephrase the question for you. Finally, move on to the next question, making a mental note to return if you have time at the end of the exam.

<u>Writers Note</u>

So dear reader, you might be a student or a learner which we are and whatever may be your age, I have made my best efforts to reveal the secrets of a genius. But the path to walk is upto you; I can only light the path.

If you have reached this page then I'm sure that now you understand that secret to awaken the genius within you is just you. You need to believe you are a genius.
All the best for your future endeavours.
If you have any feedback, suggestions do feel free to write it to me at rohit@firststepcorp.com